DUMMY'S LITTLE GIRL

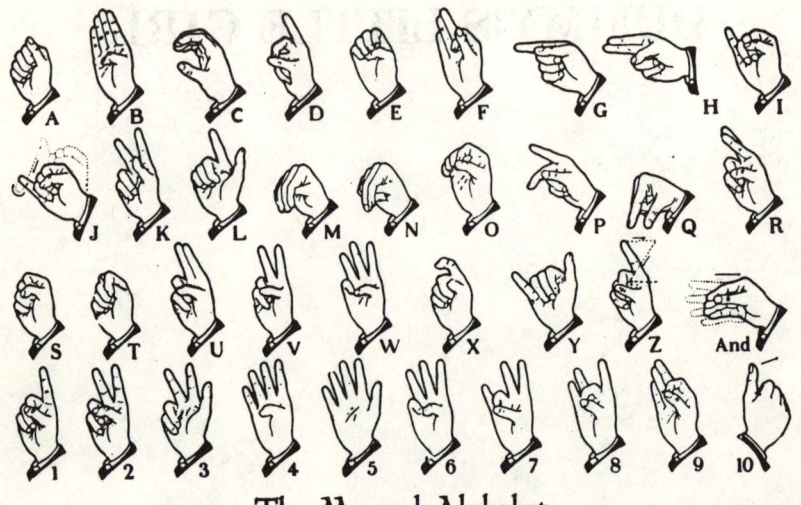

The Manual Alphabet

DUMMY'S LITTLE GIRL

by

Doris Isbell Crowe

A Hearthstone Book

Carlton Press, Inc.   New York, N.Y.

Copyright © 1993 by Doris Isbell Crowe
ALL RIGHTS RESERVED
manufactured in the United States of America
ISBN 0-8062-4623-5

*Dedicated
to
Nancy Barker
Teena Cagle
Judy Cook Pryor
and
Connor Dillard*

Thanks!

CONTENTS

Introduction by Allen Crowe ix
Foreword xi
1. In the Beginning 15
2. Mommie 20
3. BoBo: My Best Pal 28
4. Granny and Paw-Paw 31
5. Nettleton, My World of Silent Dreams 32
6. June 14, 1955, My Dad Goes Home 46
7. Another Deaf Man Enters My Life 62
8. My Mommie Goes Home 67
9. The First Ten Years (Babies) 70
10. The Second Five Years (More Babies) 86
11. College and More Dreams 96
12. Georgia On My Mind 99
13. Sleepy Hollow Road, Georgia 102
14. The Third Five Years 115
15. The Souvenir Knife 126
16. "G" 129
17. Fortieth Birthday—Grammy 133
18. Twenty-fifth Wedding Anniversary 136
19. The Thirtieth Year Tent Makers
    (More Grandbabies) 152
20. The Thirty-fifth Year, Missionaries and
    Traveling 155
21. The Beginning of the End: My 50th Birthday 158
22. HIM 162
23. "The Vision" 164
24. The Summer of '90 165
25. Louie Allen Crowe 174

26. The Second Time Around 186
27. A New World With the Hearing 189
28. Mother's Day 193
29. A Cowboy Wedding 195
30. Donna's Deaf World 197
31. The Crowe's Nest 197
    Epilogue 200

Introduction
by Allen Crowe

This is the true story of a young girl, born to parents who were deaf. The opportunity that Doris Mae Isbell McDonald-Crowe has to relive her life as a child, growing up in a small southern town in the early forties, facing all the obstacles of life, with the added burden of deaf parents provides a rare and unforgettable experience.

In "Dummy's Little Girl," Doris Crowe relates her entire life story from birth, until her present day status. It is a record of love, faith, commitment to her parents, active mother of six children (four natural, and two adopted), and thirty-five years of interpreting for a deaf spouse.

Her approach to life has exemplified a dynamic individual who has drawn many of her ideas from personal observations and experiences. Facing many obstacles that would have brought the strongest of people to their knees, she, however, due to her heritage, persevered.

Many experiences have brought her honors, via her deaf ex-husband. Being the first National Registered Interpreter for the Deaf in the state of Georgia, she has had the honor of interpreting professionally for more than forty years. Her travels have included serving in this capacity for presidents, governors, Dr. Billy Graham and numerous other dignitaries over the years.

Being reared in a "deaf world," marrying into the same environment, gave her limited opportunities to experience a "sound oriented world," until she met the man of her dreams.

This book portrays the transition of the deaf or the hearing impaired, their lives and their families, from the forties through the nineties. It also gives insight into the comparison between the two mediums. A new world emerges when "Dummy's Little Girl," marries a man who can hear and introduces her to a new element of happiness and service within the hearing world.

You will laugh, cry, feel sympathetic and often feel some empathy for the treatment of the deaf and their families of yesteryear as they endured the treatment of being regarded as second-class citizens.

Doris Crowe, has devoted her entire life of service to the hearing impaired in numerous ways. Both as a volunteer and as an employee. She was the recipient of the 1973 Penmanship of the Year Award by the state of Georgia, Department of Human Resources; Rome's Mother of the Year Award in 1983; Listed in "Who's Who" among the Leadership of America recipients in the Library of Congress in 1971. These are among the many recognitions that have been awarded to her through her efforts.

Widely known for her poetry depicting the hearing impaired, she penned the famous, "Deaf Christian's Prayer." Other writings to her credit are articles in Home Life Magazine, The New York Times and several submissions in national magazines under her pseudo writer's name.

Multi-talented, a gifted pianist and vocalist, she has utilized her God-given talents to serving in various parts of the country. Billed as "The Hi-Low's" a singing duo, she and her husband Allen continue this ministry in local nursing homes.

Standing only 4'5" tall, she has stood like a giant, while often serving as a "bridge over troubled waters" between the deaf and the hearing environments.

"Dummy's Little Girl" will give you an insight into the comparison of each world as she has penned since the inception of her first written diary at the tender age of six.

The sincerity with which the book is written will move you to tears as you follow the now 52 year old, active little woman, who once was known as "Dummy's Little Girl."

Footnote from Allen to Doris: The epithet on her father's tombstone (Dummy) Isbell reads, "To know him was to love him." This also, depicts "Dummy's Little Girl."

FOREWORD

This book is the culmination of all the diaries that I have kept over the past forty-five years. Many of you have requested that I write my memoirs. Those of you who know me personally will know that this is my first professional effort at relating my life story.

I wish to dedicate this writing to all of those individuals who have made my trek through this life more interesting and have afforded me support when it was most needed. Specific names of each person who has either directly or indirectly influenced me will not be named, as you have been told in person what you have meant to me. However, there is one person who shall remain anonymous to whom I shall always be grateful. You will find him referred to as "HIM" in this book. He was there to help in times of need and despair. Thanks much.

I wish also to remember those to whom I gave birth and nurtured to adulthood. My four natural born children and their children.

I want to make certain that my paternal grandmother, Mamie Cora Holmes Isbell, aka, Mommie receives the merit that she so justly deserves. I am sorry that I was unable to thank her enough in her lifetime for all of her teachings, and guidance to me along my way to adulthood.

Last, but by no means least, I wish to recognize all of the hearing impaired (referred to in this script as the deaf), who have been a part of my life. To my deaf parents, Carl Moorehead Isbell, Sr., and Florence Massengill Isbell, I wish to say thank you for my heritage.

I will always be careful to give all the honor, glory, and praise to Jesus, who without His guidance, I possibly could have taken other paths which might have been unbecoming to me and to my testimony.

This is my story, written from the "Crowe's Nest" located at

366 Sleepy Hollow Road in Cave Spring, Georgia. It is a nostalgic story of a little girl born in the 1940's. A monologue regarding her trials, joys, sorrows, some of her accomplishments, her transition from a deaf world into a hearing world and the drastic changes of both worlds over the past fifty-two years. It will hopefully enlighten you into the world of the deaf and their culture both of yesteryear and today.

A big thanks goes to my new husband, Allen, for his devotion, time and support in this endeavor. I love you. Shalom!

DUMMY'S LITTLE GIRL

1.
IN THE BEGINNING

"Your daddy laughs like a 'Billy Goat' and your mama talks like a chicken—Hey! Aren't you 'Dummy's Little Girl?'"

I heard those words more times than I care to remember. I could not begin to number the times that I heard that phrase as a child growing up. Almost everywhere that I went with my deaf parents, it was noticed, because they made odd sounds and talked with each other and to me on their fingers. In the early 40's this was very noticeable, as we were just as rare as midgets with the circus. We were an oddity everywhere we traveled. I became accustomed to the stares, jeers, and questioning at a very early age.

As a Christian, I know that God has a plan for every creature formed by His hands, and we as human beings do not understand many of His plans. I am a strong believer that we will probably never see the ultimate timeliness of each day until He reveals it all to us in Heaven.

Over the years, my observation has been that some people seem to have more obstacles to overcome than others. I feel that this story of my life is one of such a person. One who came into this world being different from the very beginning. One who was told very early in life by her grandmother that she was a "Special Child." One who would face and overcome more obstacles in her lifetime than the average person. One who did persevere and stand tall through trials that would have broken the common man.

The Bible begins in Genesis with "In the beginning...." Therefore since the Bible has played such an important part in my life, it seems only appropriate to begin my story in this way.

Nettleton, Mississippi is a small town located in the northern part of the state. Approximately fifteen miles south of Tupelo, the birthplace of the famous Elvis Presley. It was a farmer's town with two traffic lights, two streets containing stores, and a garment factory. My dad owned the only shoe repair shop in that little town in the mid-forties. Dad, Mommie and my Aunt Velma moved there in the fall of 1936.

Carl Moorehead Isbell, Sr. was a special man in his own right. He was a man full of wit, energy and a zest for life comparable to none. Totally deaf, he stood a mere 4'8" tall, even in his elevated shoes. Dad communicated with Mommie and other family members via utilizing the fingerspelling method. His deaf friends, however communicated with him through the American Sign Language which was used at most state schools for the deaf. His customers and the town people had to resort to the pen and pad method to make him understand. Therefore his means of interaction was somewhat limited by his deafness. This by no means deterred his outgoing personality.

May of 1938, Dad married a childhood sweetheart, Florence Dora Massengill, whom he had met at the state school for the deaf located in Jackson, Mississippi. Eleven years her senior, they had a beautiful church wedding, at Fellowship community, near Meridian, Mississippi. The Rev. Deb Stennis, a relative of the famous Statesman John Stennis, learned enough Sign Language to perform the ceremony before deaf friends and relatives who were in attendance.

There was much joy and the unusual couple were afforded all the well wishes of everyone in the communities of both Fellowship and the little township of Nettleton.

The couple left following the wedding, for North Mississippi to establish a home, knowing that they would face many trials because they were both hearing impaired and would be living in a sound oriented world away from the protection and the security of the State School for the Deaf, where both had spent most of their lives.

Mother had been born into a family of ten children. My grandfather, Pack Massengill and Granny (Mattie Nelson) were cousins. Of this union, unfortunately, there were children with sight and hearing problems. Therefore Mother had lived a more protected life than Dad. Now she, too, was leaving that security to face the world with a deaf mate.

They began their housekeeping in a small apartment across the street from the First Baptist Church of Nettleton. Mother was an active housewife. She utilized all the skills that she had gleaned from the training at the "Deaf School." She and dad also enjoyed playing Rook Cards, a game they had both learned to play at the school. Both of them made friends quickly, and often played Monopoly and other card games with couples in town who were not hearing impaired. However, their most enjoyable times were spent in visiting other deaf couples from surrounding towns. The "Deaf" are known to be very clannish and relish each other's company over that of their hearing peers. Perhaps for no other reason but to communicate in their own unique language.

Dad, known by the people in the town as "Dummy," made an adequate living repairing shoes. He did not seem to resent the name "Dummy," in fact he considered it a "Love Name." He was a very frugal man, and made every nickel count. Mother canned vegetables gathered from their garden, and kept the house as orderly as possible with their very meager furnishings.

In the spring of 1940, following a very cold and snowy winter (March 29, to be exact), I was introduced to the world of the "Deaf." All of the relatives and neighbors came to admire the tiny new addition to the "odd couple." (Later, I was always amused that people had the audacity to think that it required the ability to hear and speak to reproduce.) I was named after my Aunt Katie Mae King, and a derivative of my mother's name. Thereafter, I was known as Doris Mae, "Dummy's Little Girl." With blonde curly hair, and very petite, my big blue eyes observed every movement that my parents made. They knew immediately that I could hear, because I responded to their noises. Neither of them could make clear precise words, only guttural sound. I learned early to be very obedient and react to their gestures.

At night, Mother would pin my diaper to her gown in order to feel me squirm if I awakened and needed attention. They had no other alternative. They had a perfect child, one who could hear and eventually talk, one whose cries fell on deaf ears. She knew they would respond to her needs only by touch or visual communication. My first words were not DA-DA nor MA-MA rather they were ooohhhh or aaahhh. I learned early to squint and make faces without sounds. It was not necessary for me to cry, therefore I did not cry.

Fourteen months later (May of 1941), my brother Carl Moorehead Isbell, Jr., better known as "Bubba," was born into this little family. Immediately it fell my lot to inform Mother and Dad when "Bubba," had needs. I grew up fast at fourteen months, assuming adult responsibilities. By now I was functioning as the ears and mouth of my parents. I also assumed the role of "doorbell," "interpreter," "baby cry signal when my brother was in distress," and mother to my little brother. Naturally he rebelled at this role I played, because he considered me a peer rather than a mother. I always did my duty, loving and caring for him at all times. I had always loved babies, even at fourteen months of age.

It seemed that I had inherited the ear problems that my father had experienced as a child. I had a continuous earache and throat infections all during my childhood. Bouts of pneumonia were not uncommon. My parents comforted me the best that they knew how, and relied heavily on Dr. Dabbs, the family doctor who had delivered both of mother's babies at home. Dr. Dabbs was a kind and considerate man. He talked to me as if I were an adult, even when I was a small child.

Many of the incidents that occurred prior to my eighteenth month episode, are very vague and have been conveyed to me via relatives, Mommie and neighbors. However, when I was that age, I recall vividly the day that mother and dad placed me outside in the fenced backyard to play.

It was a spring-like day, following a rather cool night. I wanted to play, and always had a knack for entertaining myself and using my vivid imagination at play.

My parents always trusted me, because I behaved in such a "grown-up" manner, even as a tiny baby. Dad had just emptied the coal heater and the scuttle was on the back porch filled with hot coals from the fire he had made the previous night.

Seeing the pretty colors, and having never been instructed that they were dangerous, that they were hot and would be injurious to me if I touched them, I did not realize the impending danger which I was facing. I was only imagining a wonderful way to utilize all those pretty little red colored rocks in my play area. Anxious to play, I plunged both hands deep into the hot coals. My arms had been submerged up to my elbows. Immediately I withdrew them, with the outer layer of the skin from my tiny arms peeling off as I did so. Quickly, I ran to the back door. I knocked, and made faces, calling for my parents in the usual manner—ooohhhh, aaahhh. They did not respond, my cries for help fell on deaf ears. When they did not come to my aid, I ran to the fence, and stood there making faces and revealing my intense pain by emitting louder and louder sounds of my ooohhh's and aaahh's.

After a period of time, the blood began to ooze down my arms. A dear neighbor sensing something might be wrong, since she saw me playing alone, and making the awful noises, came to my rescue.

Mrs. Henry Roberts always affectionately known to Bubba and me as Aunt Gert, was devastated at the sight she saw. She began to weep. Upon seeing her tears, I too began to cry, for I thought I had possibly done something wrong and disobeyed my parents, and this would cause them to lose their trust in my ability to play alone.

Aunt Gert had no grandchildren. She had only one son, therefore I looked to her as a surrogate grandmother. A kind, godly lady, she could communicate with Mother and Dad with the old-fashioned two-hand alphabet used by the older deaf.

Immediately, Aunt Gert went to the front of the house to summon my parents and inform them of my injuries. Quickly, they ran to the back door, picked me up and looked at my burned arms and hands.

Wrapping my arms in diapers, they rushed me off to the doctor's office. He gave them instructions as to how they should care for me. The written words seemed so complicated for them to understand, they were afraid that they might make a mistake in doing so, and cause more harm than good for their little girl. They sought additional help.

Aunt Gert, then called Mommie to inform her of the accident. She and the doctor both felt that this was an unusual crisis, even for "normal people" (as Mother and Dad often referred to hearing people as normal people).

Mommie came. She, too, was a dear, God-fearing, woman. A prayer warrior who had begun to pray for me the minute she received the message regarding the mishap. Mommie made such an impact on my life that until my dying day, I will always thank God for her and the guidance she gave me. I will be compelled to thank Him for sending me someone like Mommie to love and influence my life and lead me to Christ.

2.
MOMMIE

I would be amiss if I did not pause and convey the deep feelings that I had for Mommie. I was always moved by her dependence on the Lord for everything. A day never passed that she knelt by her bed and prayed for each child, grandchild, in-law, neighbor, pastor, and churches, all by name. Her own personal needs were requested last. I recall too, how she would take me to the bathroom, and we would kneel beside the toilet to ask the Lord for forgiveness when I had done something wrong. This was when she felt I should ask the Lord for forgiveness for committing a grave misdeed.

Mommie had not led an easy life. Widowed at thirty four, her young husband had been swept away from her as a result of the ravages of the swine flu. Leaving her with six young children ranging in age from twelve years to six months. An enormous task lay ahead for a young woman who had no marketable skills at earning a living. With no life insurance, and very few worldly goods, she managed well.

Dad was Mommie and Poppa's third child, the third son. At the age of two, he fought a bout with the whooping cough, complicated by measles and rickets simultaneously. Mommie was not to be beaten. Daily she transported her baby boy by bus to the doctors in Birmingham. Seeking aid for her ailing son, she thought he would surely die. This is what increased her faith in God. She had no one else to depend on at that time.

When the crisis had ceased, the extremely high temperatures had left my father with a total hearing loss, never to be regained in his entire lifetime.

As the result of his hearing loss, it was explained to Mommie in lay terms the severity of his handicapping condition. The eighth nerve that serves as a communication/interpretation mechanism to the brain is very fragile, and elevated temperatures can cause them to be irreparably burned. It is similar to a telephone when the wires are disconnected. A person may possess a perfectly good telephone, but if it is not connected to the incoming line, it will not convey sound. So it was with my Dad's ears.

He possessed a brilliant mind, and perfect eardrums, but the wires (nerves) had been severed thereby obstructing the information being transmitted to the brain from the ears. His deafness never affected him psychologically, however the illness left him with a stunted growth, resulting in a small stature. He was only 4'8" tall.

Mommie searched for ways to educate all of her children. "Little Carl," as he was affectionately known to all the family members, was her very first challenge. She taught him in all of the social graces, and potty trained him as she did the others.

When he reached six years of age, she placed him on a train to attend the Alabama State School for the Deaf located in Talladega, Alabama. She did this reluctantly, because he was so tiny for his age. However she knew he could derive a better education there, than under her tutelage. There he could learn a trade, designed for the deaf and could become a productive citizen in the future. This is what she hoped and prayed for all of her children.

Talladega was over one hundred and twenty miles away from Birmingham, Alabama. "Little Carl" would leave for school each year, in September, then return home for the Christmas Holidays. He would then board the train, and upon arrival at the school remain there until it closed in May of the following year. Adjusting well he made numerous deaf friends while there. Many of his friends would visit him in Birmingham when he was at home during the holidays, or in the summer. These visits from friends helped keep him from being lonely at home.

At the tender age of eight, his dad, who owned a small community grocery store in Birmingham, died. Mommie gathered her little brood and journeyed to Houlka, Mississippi to reside with her parents. Grandma and Grandpa Holmes lived near the Harris family, therefore they could give them odd jobs to do. This was their only means of survival. Mommie wanted to raise her children right and see to it that they acquired the education that she desired for them.

In the fall, "Little Carl," was sent to the Mississippi State School for the Deaf in Jackson, Mississippi, to continue his education. His older brothers, George and Howard, assisted their mother in raising his younger sisters Jean, Katie and Velma, and providing for his needs at the school.

Many of his summers were spent working in the fields near Houlka. The entire family worked together to survive. Any means for earning money to support the family, was a challenge for all of them.

"Little Carl" remained at the school until he was seventeen years of age and in the eleventh grade. He had been training in the Vocational Department as a Shoe Repairman. A skilled mechanic, he possessed an innate ability to follow directions, and the school officials were confident that he would do well in the work force.

There was one sister left at home at this time, therefore he felt compelled to leave school and seek full-time employment because Mommie needed him for financial support. He left the school reluctantly but obediently. He never received the diploma that had always been a dream for him, since he was a small tot in Alabama.

A job opportunity became available in Aberdeen, Mississippi, so they moved. He began his work as an apprentice in a shoe repair shop. Mommie had never worked outside of the home. She had, however, used her skills to do ironing, sewing and other odd jobs to sustain her family. A skilled seamstress, she quilted and crocheted for the more affluent ladies in the community. Her children had gone their separate ways, as they aged enough to leave the nest. "Little Carl," however, needed Mommie and she needed him. She had always felt a special closeness to him because of his handicapping condition.

Several years later, an opportunity arose, when a traveling

Neolite heels salesman from Memphis informed Dad and Mommie that the owner of the shoe repair shop in nearby Nettleton was planning to retire, Mommie prayed about the golden opportunity afforded them. Informing Dad in sign language that this was an answer to her prayer, they journeyed to Nettleton to survey the possibilities.

The town was located approximately twenty miles from Aberdeen. Nearby were other members of the family. It would be an ideal location for him to continue his trade, and possibly in the future build a home.

Being aware of little Florence at the School for the Deaf, knowing also that eventually she would give him up to her, Mommie recommended that they make a loan at the local bank and take the plunge together, literally "hand in hand."

Faithfully, Mommie assisted her son in his business. She interpreted for him when the customers came into the shoe shop. During the slack hours, she would crochet and sew. One of the items that she began to crochet was a "Wagon Wheel" bedspread for "Little Carl's" first born. Ironically, it was completed only a few months prior to my birth. (I have since passed this heirloom to my only daughter in hopes that she too will give it on to one of her children.)

Business was good, even during the war years. Rubber was scarce, and shoes were kept for longer periods of time. Dad's skill at repairing shoes was known far and wide. People in neighboring towns would bring their worn shoes to town on Saturdays when they came to do their shopping. They would then pick them up the following Saturday, as they made their weekly trek to town. Therefore, Saturday was Dad's busiest day.

Dad continued to make friends. He was a clown, loved children, acted like a little boy at times and made children laugh. He was unique and he knew it.

Mommie assisted Dad in purchasing a small Willis automobile. This is when he began to make regular visits to M.S.D. in Jackson. Mommie knew that wedding plans were in the making as soon as "Little Florence" completed her studies at the school. She knew also that she must seek another home. Mommie was filled with mixed emotions, but she had always wanted what was best for my Dad.

During the years Mommie had been a great inspiration to Dad, and his success in the business relied heavily on her influence. He knew this, but Mommie was not the kind of person to accept accolades or take credit for merit rightfully belonging to others.

So when Dad and Mother married, Mommie moved on to her other "Mission in Life," to help others.

Upon mother's arrival in Nettleton, she assisted Dad in the shoe repair shop.

She too made friends. Mother was a hard worker and a good help mate. Surprisingly enough, she adjusted well in her new environment, far away from the farm and the confines of the school for the deaf.

She was special to my Dad.

Following the wedding ceremony, Mommie moved from one child's home to another. Not wanting to be a burden to any one person, usually the time that she visited, was when she was needed the most. Often it was the birth of a grandchild or an illness in the family that she would be summoned on the spur of the moment to make her move. Moving was not a chore, because all of her worldly belongings were either stored away in her trunk or suitcase. These followed her wherever she went.

Therefore the need arising, Mommie was asked to come and help mother care for me. The day following my calamity, she arrived with her purse in one hand and her Bible in the other. Her trunk and suitcase were on the back of Uncle Marvin Haney's truck. Entering with a willingness to do all that she could, she let it be known that she was also armed with her prayers.

Her first project was to inform all of the people in the neighborhood that she was in dire need of egg whites to aid in the healing process of "Doris Mae's little hands and arms."

Everyone who had been informed of the tragedy responded. Daily as the neighbors and women in town prepared their meals, they would set aside the whites of the eggs specifically for her. Dad would go by and fetch most of them. However others would deliver their own, mainly just to observe my progress and bring small gifts to cheer me. Mommie's skillful efforts to assist in the healing process were of course aided by her prayers.

I recall vividly how she would soothe the painful sores by mixing the whites with baking soda, then gently pat the mixture on my seared arms and hands. Wrapping them loosely in soft cloth diapers, she would instruct me not to remove them. This was done three times daily. Each time she removed the wraps, she would look at my badly burned hands, look toward heaven then pray. I can still hear her prayers for my hands. "Lord! Let little Doris Mae's hands and arms heal. I dedicate them to You for her. I am sure she will use them for Your glory. I ask this if it is Your perfect will that there be no scars left there. Let her hands be nimble to talk to her deaf parents, play a piano, draw, write, sew, cook, wash dishes and do all the things that other little girls do. Lord, do this in Jesus' name."

Then she would cry. I could not understand why she cried each time she removed the wraps. It was difficult for me to understand her tears. Thinking she was in pain also, I too would cry.

Following her prayer, she would sing, "Amazing Grace," smile, lift her hands toward heaven then "Thank the Lord." This I could really not understand. I thought that she was thanking him for my being in pain.

Over the years, she related the story to me numerous times. She said that as my hands began to heal, my fingers and palms began to atrophy. She immediately began to administer some paregoric prior to removing the wraps. Holding my hands up she would ask me to move my fingers. It must have been very painful, for I would grimace. Mommie continued to pray and touch each blister and ask the Lord for removal of the scars.

Months later, when the blisters were gone, she began physical therapy. I was taught the Manual Alphabet utilized by the deaf. I learned to spell words. Making a game out of it, I found it was fun to learn. As I said before, Mommie was a born teacher.

As my dear grandmother worked with my hands each day, she would sing hymns to me and rub my back until I fell asleep. I can still hear her voice in the corridors of my mind, singing and praying for my "little hands."

I could follow her tunes perfectly, however, I did not make any effort to talk. Emulating the sounds that my parents made, my fingers would spell the words and the gyrations and grimaces on my face would convey my needs to them. I felt no need to talk.

The following Christmas, Mother and Dad gave me a little piano, which had been ordered from the Sears-Roebuck Catalog. I was two at the time. Mommie would follow the directions and I learned to play some of the familiar tunes she had sung to me while I was ill. She could play some songs by ear, so with this new toy that I had acquired, I immediately began to use my fingers more.

Accompanying the music by humming along, "Jesus Loves Me," I learned to listen to the tones of the music. However, I would not sing, neither would I talk. Those ooohhhh and aaahhh words were the only ones I knew. Springtime came. The relatives who had farms needed Mommie to watch the babies. She left me once again to aid those who needed her most. With purse, Bible, trunk, and suitcase in hand, she left to do her so called "Mission Work."

I loved my piano. On some days my voice was the only audible sound that I heard in my house, other than Bubba's crying. Placing the piano on the dresser, I would stand in a chair, look in the mirror, smile and make faces at myself. Mommie had taught me to look at the sunlight or a light when I entered a room. Prior to greeting people, she would instruct me to look up then smile. She said that my eyes were bluer that way. My smile was to attract the attention of anyone in the room. Until this day, fifty-two years later, I am still programmed to smile, look up, show my teeth, then thank the Lord for my hearing and my voice.

At age four, Mommie came to stay with us again. Chronic earaches and a siege of pneumonia had been the purpose of calling her to our aid. She seemed to be the only one who could appease me with the warmed salt bags placed on my ears. Rubbing my back and singing to me also served as a tranquilizer for the pain that I endured. Oft times she would request that my father blow smoke into my ears.

The town drunk, hearing of my plight, even recommended warm urine, (which surprisingly enough, worked). Fortunately, Mommie used that remedy sparingly and only as a last resort. She would try anything at least once. During this particular visit, I recall Mommie teaching me to read. My parents were avid readers and enjoyed solving cross word puzzles. She used the daily newspaper to teach me the printed word . . . so I can truthfully say, the vast majority of my early vocabulary was derived from the Tupelo Daily Journal.

Mother and Dad relied heavily on the printed word, therefore they always had ample pencils and paper on hand. The Neolite salesman who had earlier befriended Dad, always brought him samples of advertisement pads. Ironically, among one of the first words that I learned to read and write was Neolite.

Mommie's formal education consisted of an eighth grade education. However, she possessed numerous talents and skills. She made efforts to pass these on to me. Teaching me new words daily the very first difficult word that I recall mastering was the word "refrigerator." She would require me to enunciate each word, and each phrase. She would not allow me to "Butcher the King's English." At that time, I thought that was most important. Not understanding what she meant, I thought she was referring to my Aunt Katie Mae King who owned a grocery store near Memphis. Thinking fully that I was to emulate those who were from the "Big City," I followed her tutelage carefully.

In the meantime, Dad entered a cross-word puzzle contest. The first prize being awarded was a Webster's Collegiate Dictionary. With the assistance of a friend and neighbor, Croom Armour, they won that monstrosity for me. Upon receiving the huge book, I began to pore over its contents like a new toy. Mommie took the time to explain the new words and explain its contents. I learned to pronounce words that I had never even heard spoken.

It was during this particular visit that Mommie encouraged Mother and Dad to take us to the local Methodist Church. She taught me the song "This Little Light of Mine," and "Let the Son Shine In." She, too, taught me to become self confident and to overcome the fear of standing before an audience.

I recall standing on the piano stool at the church, with no fear whatsoever, and singing those songs to the top of my lungs. I remember also viewing the congregation and watching my deaf parents as they observed each movement of the mouth of their dear daughter. I knew each note and sound was falling on their deaf ears. Nevertheless they applauded each time I completed a song. The members of the congregation would smile, because they knew how proud this deaf couple was of their hearing child.

They would sit patiently during the sermon, never hearing or knowing one single word that our pastor had spoken. They always bowed their heads when the others did, and mouthed the words when the Amen was said.

Time moved on and so did Mommie. I became stronger each day and continued to play my little piano and sing my songs she had so carefully taught me. Mother and Dad continued to take Bubba and me to church without Mommie. I would hold the song book in my hand, and point to the words as they were sung by the choir and congregation. They also followed along with the group when the Responsive Reading was read. I remember accompanying my parents to the bank at the tender age of four, to discuss with the President of the Bank, the possibility of securing a loan to purchase a small plot of ground to erect a little four room house behind Uncle Pipe and Aunt Gert. While at the bank, little did I realize that this would be the first of thousands of experiences that would be mine over the years to interpret for deaf people. By now my hands were miraculously healed and being used in many ways. Very few tell-tale scars remained from that frightful day that I saw the beautiful burning embers so enticing to a little girl of deaf parents.

3.
BOBO: MY BEST PAL

It was during this time that I recall true loneliness. I had no little friends with whom to play, other than my little brother. Sundays would often bring cousins to visit. Most of them were either boys or older girls. Mother and Dad would also have visitors who were deaf like them. Many of their friends did not have children either. Therefore, I had no other choice but to play alone.

As innovative children will do, I began to play with an imaginary playmate.

She was a good playmate, and never did anything wrong. She also never instructed me to do wrong things. Her hair was black and she had dark eyes and playing with her was an enjoyable time of my life. I gave her the unusual name of "BoBo."

"BoBo" taught me many things about life. She always told me to dream of better times. She always told me to be proud of my parents, even though they were deaf. Pride was instilled in me by my little imaginary friend. She helped me to learn to like my name, to be proud of my heritage, and to shoot for the stars in everything that I did.

"BoBo" was always with me at night, insisting that I say my prayers daily, she would tell me that she was a special friend and that she would never leave me, until there was someone else to take her place. I loved "BoBo," she was special and filled many lonely hours.

I was never afraid of the dark, simply because "BoBo" was there. She told me stories of far away lands and beautiful islands. A world traveler. She had been to all of these places, and encouraged me to make that one of my dreams. "BoBo" was like me, she was not deaf.

The summer of 1945, at age five, I recall playing outside in the backyard of our new little house. Bubba did not play dolls, so therefore I had a difficult time coercing him into playing with me, however on this day, I had been successful in doing so.

Mother was inside the house cleaning, as my younger brother and I sneaked into the kitchen to retrieve some leftover cooked oatmeal from the refrigerator. After placing the food in glass cereal bowls, we proceeded outside to play "house." Mother's sixth sense would often warn her if we were into mischief, however, this day, we eluded her watchful eyes.

Mother's prized "oatmeal bowls," the kind that were a hidden treasure within the oatmeal boxes, were now on our makeshift tables behind the house. Inadvertently my bowl overturned spilling the contents on the brick walk. It broke into two large pieces. Trying to hide my faux-pas, I slipped on the slimy substance and fell.

Simultaneously, mother came to the door to see that we were playing and were not into any type of trouble.

Oblivious to any household noise, and our presence undetected, she had not seen her two little ones take "forbidden" food outside. She knew instantly that something was wrong. I had cut my foot, which was very small anyway, from the tip of my little toe to the end of my heel. I knew that it was a very deep cut because of the pain and also that it was bleeding profusely.

Bubba, fearful that he would be blamed, pointed to me and to the blood. By this time, the step revealed a large pool of blood.

Mother began to panic. I motioned to her that it was my foot. By this time, we were all in tears, at the gaping wound. She instructed Bubba to go inside the house and gather towels to wrap my foot. Obediently, he responded to her sign language.

Wrapping my foot, she directed Bubba to hold the towel around my foot. She began to clean the area, so as not to startle Dad when he arrived. Her plan was to carry me in her arms to Aunt Gert's house.

In the meantime, Dad arrived home. Seeing all of the doors open, blood splattered outside in the backyard, and drops of blood throughout the house leading to Aunt Gert's, he began to cry. He could not imagine what had happened to his family.

Instinctively, he drove to the doctor's office. There we were, all of us, and "Dummy's Little Girl," propped in a chair with Dr. Dabbs stitching up the wound. He gave me the responsibility of counting the stitches. There were 65 in all. All because I wanted to play house with oatmeal.

The doctor informed mother and dad at that time, that when the wound healed, that I would probably walk with a limp the remainder of my life, due to the severed tendons and loss of muscle in the area.

Mommie was called once again to pray, nurture, do her Missionary Work and aid in my recovery. Immediately, she began to use some of her homemade remedies to assist in the healing process. Of course, physical therapy as we know it today, did not exist, but Mommie was the teacher, and she knew exactly what to do . . . and she did it!

Due to her massages, insisting that I put pressure on my foot when it hurt, moving my foot in warm water for hours, I recovered. A limp is not detected as I walk today. Her guidance was from the Great Physician, and through her daily prayers. Her prayer was that I would not be dually handicapped. Those prayers were heard and answered.

I don't recall ever taking another bowl into the yard. As a result of the accident, some of the neighbors purchased me a plastic tea set, and other items to assist in my play area. These were my toys thereafter.

Bubba and I continued to play together. One day he informed me that the town of Nettleton had purchased a new fire truck. We asked if we could go see the big new truck and hear the siren.

Dad took us to see the monstrosity. It was very pretty, and appeared to be a very serviceable piece of equipment.

However, there had been no fires lately for the truck to be used. One fall day, several months following the purchase of the large, siren laden truck, a fire mysteriously occurred in the large grassy field adjacent to Aunt Gert and Uncle Pipe's house. We were eating supper at the time, therefore Dad and Mother did not hear the siren. BUT . . . Bubba and I did. We were excited. We knew Jimmy Rogers would be driving the big vehicle.

We motioned to mother and dad that there was a fire. And Oh! to our surprise, it was next door. We stood in awe as the firemen poured the water from the large hose and extinguished the blazing grass. Later, to our dismay, there was another fire inside our house, two little children's pants were set afire by blistering hands of deaf parents.

4.
GRANNY AND PAW-PAW

Granny and Paw-Paw resided near Meridian. They were cousins and due to that lineage, they produced several children with handicapping conditions of the ears and eyes.

Ten children were born to the family. The boys, J.L.; Shep; Bill; and Lamar had some form of albinoism. The girls Nannie, Enolia, Eva Ruth, Winnie, Mary, and mother had hearing problems.

My grandparents were typical farmers in the southlands during the depression. They raised vegetables and farm crops yearly. Very religious people, they were a close-knit family.

My first recollection of going to the farm resulted in a trip to the corn crib. I had never seen so many varmints convened in one place in my life. Afterward, I did not volunteer to fetch the corn.

Bathing on the farm was another experience. Following the wash-day every Saturday, the rinse water was left in the tub to heat in the sun. It was then taken into the wash-shed where one little city girl could climb in and bathe in the wash tub. I dare not use the lye soap that was furnished.

One day, twin cousins, Jean put Joan and the cat in the well bucket and lowered her into the well. We were curious as to what was in the confines of the water hole. Realizing that we had made a mistake, since we could not pull her out alone, we had to call for help. The cat fell out and drowned in the melee. Joan was retrieved unharmed. However, a new well had to be dug as a result of that little escapade.

I often wondered if that is where they got the idea that curiosity killed the cat . . . it sure did that one!

5.
NETTLETON, MY WORLD OF SILENT DREAMS

We had wonderful neighbors in the little town of Nettleton. The Cheeks lived across the street from us and they had a teenage daughter named Tommie Jean. She had a BIG piano. I loved Miss Erdis (Mrs. Cheek) and her mode of stylishness. She was of a dying breed of Southern Ladies. The epitome of beauty, she was also very sweet to me. I recall my very first birthday party. She had invited all of the children in and around the town to my fifth birthday celebration. Decorating her dining room with an umbrella turned upside down and hanging from the chandelier, she had it filled with gifts, various and sundry things that I could use as I started to school in the fall. I had so much fun that day that I do believe I felt that a small part of heaven was bestowed upon me that day.

Tommie Jean could play the piano. She taught me about recitals and told me all about piano teachers. She talked of Ole Miss and the music department that was located there. She showed me pictures of grand pianos at the college and told me of New York and its symphony orchestra. She had never been to "The Big Apple," but had heard others speak of it. Each summer, I enjoyed spending time with her and listening to her stories. If Mother and Dad couldn't find me, they sure didn't have to look far, because it was a sure bet I was across the street learning more about the piano and Tommie Jean teaching me to play Stardust by Hoagy Carmichael. This teenager even had music that came from Hollywood. What seemed so incredible was that she was able to read all of the notes on the sheet music. I wanted to learn to do that.

She taught me the piano keyboard, and I taught her to finger spell so she could talk to my deaf parents. We taught each other.

School began for me in the fall of 1946. I was scheduled to enter the first grade in elementary school that year. Miss King was scheduled to be my first grade teacher. Upon arriving at school I met more children than I had ever seen in my entire life. They made fun of me because I talked on my fingers and would not talk much. I began to cry, and the school personnel called Dad. He came to the school to demonstrate how intelligent I was. The Superintendent decided at that time to move me across the hall with the older children into the second grade.

I was envious of most of those in attendance because they had the opportunity of riding to school on the bus. Some of them rode twenty miles one way. I had to walk. However I would walk with Tommie Jean, and on the way of the ten block trek, various other children would join our clan. Ultimately, when we arrived at school, there would be all ages of boys and girls in our little entourage.

This is the year I met Judy Cook. Judy has remained a lifelong friend that I named my only daughter after. Judy's father was a painter having moved to Nettleton from the Gulf coast. He had been employed at Ingalls Shipyards. I had never seen the ocean, so when she mentioned it, that was something foreign to me. Aunt Toy (Judy's mother), operated one of the two beauty shops in town. She was a lovely lady and looked for the world like Dale Evans. I loved Uncle Orville and Aunt Toy. An only child, Judy would often ask if I could accompany them on trips. I recall my very first trip to the "Big City." It was with the Cook's in their big Pontiac car.

My dad had traded the Willis for an Army Jeep he had salvaged from the Army Salvage Depot. He had made little seats and wooden doors to make it more comfortable. Orange was the color he chose to paint his new acquisition. I wasn't ashamed of it. It rode well, and was known everywhere as "Dummy's jeep." Therefore, when I went with Judy, it was a real treat to ride in a big automobile.

When I entered school, many of the children did not understand why my parents could not talk. Judy soon learned to fingerspell, too, so she could communicate with my parents. She was a friend who took the extra time to talk with my parents. She, too, was not afraid of them. I suppose that is why I loved her so dearly.

Often children can be cruel. They called me "Dummy's Little Girl." Some would tease me and say that my daddy could hear if he would clean out his ears. One such incident occurred on the school playground at recess. We were playing softball and I was up at bat. The guy on first base was a third grader. He yelled and made that statement. I was enraged, hit the ball with all my might then ran for first base with nothing else in mind but to take a bite out of his leg. I did so with all the gusto that I could muster. That was the only time that I can recall being taken to the Principal's office.

I was not spanked, but was required to go home for the remainder of the day. My only remorse was that it had been so humiliating to me to miss my spelling class because of that "dummy."

I loved school, but most of all, I loved acting in the operettas and performing in the music recitals. Mrs. McClanahan was my music teacher. I loved every minute of my music lessons. I would arrive at home after school each day, do my homework, then run across the road and practice my music at Tommie Jean's house.

I did not have a big piano of my own, but I had dreams of owning one some day. I talked to Dad, and he said that as soon as I reached the third grade, I would be old enough to go with Uncle Pipe and the others to pick cotton. He made a deal with me. He said if I paid for half of the price of the piano, he would pay for the other half. I began to save my quarters.

Aunt Gert and Uncle Pipe always gave me a quarter whenever I made straight A's on my report card. Therefore I had quite a few in my bank. I enjoyed school and all of the activities, but most of all I enjoyed learning. I also enjoyed reading and spent many of my summers reading books and studying that Webster's Collegiate Dictionary.

Saturdays were busy times for me, too. Mother, Bubba and I would rise early, heat the water inside the house then take it out to the "smoke house" to do the weekly wash. We were always finished by lunch time. After lunch we would go to town to the "Shoe Shop" where we would assist Dad with the many customers who came into town that day. I recall one Saturday that my Uncle Howard (my father's brother from Shannon), came to visit. Riley's store was on the corner, just two doors down from Dad's shop. Uncle Howard asked if I wanted an ice cream cone. Naturally I did.

We walked over to the store where several men were sitting around the coke box. Uncle Howard picked me up, sat me on the box and said "now work for your ice cream. I want you to fingerspell the alphabet with your fingers as rapidly as you can." Well, I began to oblige him. Upon completion of my task, I made the sign for ice cream.

Inquiring as to what the gesture was, I told him that was my payment. Thereafter, each time I passed Mr. Riley's store, if there were any new folks in town, they always called "Dummy's Little Girl" in there to show how fast her fingers could move. Guess what! I would inevitably get an ice cream afterward.

Saturday nights, following a very strenuous day at the shop, my Dad and Mother would play cards or other games with people in the community. This was an enjoyable time of my life, too.

My friends always talked on Mondays of listening to the Grand Ole Opry on the radio on Saturday nights. Often I would visit friends and listen with awe to Dell Wood as she played the piano. That instilled in me the desire to try harder at playing the piano.

I had another dream, too. I told Dad that I knew that every Saturday night that boxing was held at the Madison Square Garden in New York City. If he would buy a radio, I could interpret the play by play, blow by blow for him LIVE and he would not have to wait and read about it in the Sports Section of the Daily Journal. This really impressed my Dad. Surprisingly enough in a few weeks we had a radio. I was ecstatic. There was live music, sound, voices, words and many other things on that radio that filled my lonely days. It was not so quiet around the house after that innovative idea.

At the end of my first year in school, I had numerous absences due to earaches and sore throats. Dr. Dabbs recommended to Mother and Dad that I have my tonsils removed when school closed. I was then whisked off to the hospital to have surgery.

I suppose because Mother and Dad were deaf and did not understand, they chose not to remain with me. The hospital stay lasted for one week. The nurses took care of me, and Dad and Mother came to visit about one hour once a day. I was terrified and so alone. I could not believe that there was so much sickness and death all around me. I also did not realize that this was the first of many hospitalizations that I would encounter in my lifetime.

Near the end of my third year in school, two weeks prior to my eighth birthday, I became gravely ill. Regurgitating and experiencing extreme stomach pains, Mother administered a hefty dose of Pepto-Bismol and sent dad to tell the doctor. His orders were for me to remain in bed. Mother was now working at the local garment factory. Fearing to leave her work, she called for Mommie to come. Daily she cared for me. However, I showed no improvement. My condition worsened. From Monday until Thursday, I could not retain any food in my stomach. When Friday arrived, Mommie insisted that the doctor come once again to check me. Arriving around five p.m., his examination revealed that I had acute appendicitis. It would be necessary for me to be hospitalized. Immediately my Dad took me to the hospital. Perhaps due to his deafness, he felt I was in good hands, therefore he left me. I was all alone in a hospital full of strangers facing major surgery. But I knew I had to be strong for my Dad.

At eight o'clock that night, I was in surgery and an appendectomy was performed. However during the procedure the appendix ruptured resulting in peritonitis. I remained in the hospital that time for three weeks, very very ill. I was unable to swallow, and as with the last hospitalization, my parents only visited one hour each day.

My Uncle Howard came by twice a day. He was like a second father to me and gave me much comfort.

Mommie was beginning to age and they did not want to subject her to too many responsibilities, therefore she remained at Uncle Howard's and prayed for me. After three weeks of hospitalization, I returned home. Two days later, I began to hemorrhage. My folks called the doctor only to be told not to worry, that I had just become a little woman. Neither my mother, Mommie nor anyone had ever explained such things to me. Was I ever more in for a surprise when the birds and the bees, and "Little Women," came into my life at the tender age of eight.

The summer found me visiting with my Granny Massengill again. That was quite an experience as I was not accustomed to farm life with no toilet facilities nor running water. I was afraid of spiders, snakes, mice and the like. They all seemed to be plentiful on that farm and they would invariably want to make an appearance when I was around. My twin cousins Jean and Joan Massengill (my mother's brother, Uncle J.L.'s daughters), entertained me. Uncle J.L. had an old A Model Ford. Those girls were always amused when I came for a visit because I would pack a roll of toilet tissue and a bag of sugar in my suitcase. The purpose of the tissue was that Granny did not provide such luxuries in the outhouse, and I could not force myself to use the Sears-Roebuck Catalog which was provided or the seasoned corn cobs made available for cleaning purposes.

During this visit, I was under the impression that the catalog was reading material. I took it up to the house with me to read only to discover numerous pages were missing. However, it still made for interesting reading material. Later, to my dismay, I heard Granny calling my name from afar. She was in the outhouse. I ran down to discover that she was disgruntled that I had removed her cleaning material. I was then instructed to leave the catalog there and never remove it from the coat hanger provided just for that purpose.

Aunt Enolia and Aunt Eva Ruth, two of my mother's sisters, lived in town. They usually let me visit a couple of days with them. Bud, Tack, Ann Elizabeth, and little Bubba usually informed the other kids about my skill at fingerspelling and playing the piano. Enterprise was about the size of Nettleton, therefore I felt at home.

Anywhere I went, I always wanted to play any instrument that was available. Granny had an old pump organ, and Jean and Joan would get under the organ and pump while I played the keys. I was too small to reach the bellows and play simultaneously. That was a weird sight, but it was fun. It was much more fun than playing doctor, which they always wanted to play, and I did not. (Ironically, Jean and Joan both eventually became Registered Nurses).

Mother's other sister, Aunt Nannie, had a son my age. Bert was one of my favorite people. He was smart. He and I had many things in common. I also just liked his companionship.

Aunt Nannie had a piano. A beautiful piano, a small spinet. Uncle Ethelbert Barksdale Jones enjoyed listening to me play, and I savored every minute of tinkling the ivories for him. He could hear me play.

Uncle 'B was a rural mail carrier and Aunt Nannie was a housewife. She taught me many things about social life and whenever I would visit them, she would invite all of the little girls in the neighborhood to have tea parties on the lawn. She believed in socializing, dressing up and keeping the old Southern traditions alive. I suppose I learned to like lemonade and fried chicken at Aunt Nannie's house. That was about the only place that I had an opportunity to have the pulley-bone or a breast of chicken. Surprisingly enough, that meant much to a little girl of eight.

Also, I enjoyed being around hearing adults. Their family life was so much different than mine. There was always noise and sounds around, much unlike my household. I felt that I was near heaven when I visited there in Shubuta, Mississippi.

The fall before the third grade, I asked Uncle Pipe if he would allow me to pick cotton in his field that year. He reminded me that I was not tall enough to reach the cotton stalks, much less pull the one hundred pound bags that he provided.

I begged him to let me pick so I could earn enough money to buy the piano I wanted so badly.

Overhearing my pleas to him, Aunt Gert intervened and volunteered to assist me. She and Mommie got their heads together, rummaged through the old quilt box and gathered enough material to make me a little cotton sack. It was stitched with heavy thread and made from several old flour sacks. It was equipped to hold approximately twenty five pounds of cotton when it was filled.

Cotton picking time arrived and I was ready on the first Saturday morning of the announced day. I picked the dried hulls clean with the soft cotton placed in my little sack. They called my sack the "gunny sack."

Each day, I would pick cotton until dark. On school afternoons, I would accompany the neighbors who would pile on the pick-up truck bed and head straight for the cotton patch. I wasn't interested in having fun, I was interested in making money for a piano. That was my dream.

Each night I would count my money. I now had all of $15.00 in my piggy bank. Coins that had been collected from Mommie, Aunt Gert, Uncle Pipe, Mother and Dad for presenting a good report card.

Late one afternoon, after picking cotton all day, I was trudging home with my little sack on my shoulders. As I entered the pasture from Uncle Pipe's I heard music. It was coming from our house. I knew immediately it was not the radio, and it was not from the Cheeks. I began to run as fast as my tired little feet would carry me. It definitely was music, piano music. But, "Where did that thing come from?"

As I stepped up on the porch, I heard Tommie Jean laugh and point to Dad as she began the strains of the old favorite, "Stardust."

Immediately, I ran into the house and stood in the middle of the floor in amazement. There was MY piano. At last, I had a musical instrument of my very own to play.

It was the most beautiful, big, old, upright, monstrosity that I had ever seen. It had no stool. One leg was missing as a result of having survived the Tupelo tornado years earlier.

Tommie Jean was perched in a chair playing her heart out. I began to cry. She stood and said, "It's all yours." I sat down and began to play my piano.

Even though I was exhausted from picking the balls of cotton all day, even though my fingers had bled from being pricked by the dried leaves; even though the chair was too low; I played the piano all night.

I could do that. I did not disturb anyone, because the music that I played had always fallen on my parents' deaf ears. I was so very happy.

The fifth grade found me in a year of crisis. My mother had become very ill, and had to be hospitalized. Surgery was required, and in the process of the procedure, the doctor inadvertently punctured her bladder. Mother, being deaf, did not understand what was happening to her body. She thought she had a malignancy. Mother remained in the hospital for two weeks, then was brought home.

She was not the same person that I had known previously. She began to have terrible mental outbursts, threatening to kill me. I was terrified. This was not the mother I once knew.

Mommie came to stay with us once again. Times were hard, because we had begun to rely on mother's income from the factory. Eventually, following a very tragic accident, mother had to be transferred to the state mental institution in Jackson, Miss. My heart was broken. Thanksgiving was nearing and I could not visualize the holidays without my mother. It seemed as if she had died. Judy and Aunt Toy and of course Mommie and Aunt Gert were a great consolation to me at that time. Later, the neighbors all brought a turkey and the trimmings for our Thanksgiving dinner. Our real desire was to visit mother, but the distance to the state hospital prohibited us from making the trip.

Christmas was nearing and I knew that mother was not doing well. The doctors had written to Dad and informed him that they were administering shock treatments to her. I did not understand everything that was being discussed, but overhearing the conversation between Uncle Howard and Mommie, I knew it must be something awful.

I prayed ever so hard for my mother. My deaf mother who was in a hearing environment and no one to interpret for her.

She had deaf friends but no one on the staff could understand and meet her psychological needs. I was so helpless and too far away to help her.

Christmas came and several of the townspeople brought monetary gifts and enough money for us to make the trip to visit mother and take her presents. The most memorable gift that I received that year came from Judy and her mother. They arrived on Christmas Eve for a visit. It was not very cold, and they chit-chatted for a while. Bringing a large basket of fruit, some gowns and underthings for my mother, some underwear for Bubba and Dad, and stockings for Mommie, I felt as if Santa had really come to life. Then I was given my gifts. One was a beautiful red dress. It was the first store bought dress that I had ever owned. Sequins were sewn on it and it was so very pretty. Also there was a small box with "Riley's" Jewelry store inscription on the top. Judy had beautiful jewelry, but I did not have any. My heart was beating so fast that I could hardly open the daintily wrapped box. Groping at the wrapping for several minutes I did finally succeed in tearing the paper off to reveal the most beautiful ring I had ever seen in my life. They both knew that I loved Dogwood flowers, because of its Christian significance. The sterling silver ring was a dogwood flower. Without a doubt, it was the most beautiful gift I had ever received in my entire life. Crying I placed the ring in the box. Immediately, Aunt Toy, stated that the ring was given to wear and I should not take it off.

The gift was to be a remembrance of a new life and better days were ahead for all of us.

I placed the ring on my finger and never took it off until I replaced it with a wedding band. Placing it in my jewelry box to wear only on special occasions, it still graces my jewelry box. I still remember very vividly, as a ten year old, that cool December night in 1950, when kindly neighbors brought Christmas to a broken hearted deaf family in north Mississippi.

We visited mother that Christmas. We were loaded with gifts for her from her many friends and relatives. These were not important, she was angry with us for not taking her home. I was so sad that we could not take her out of that awful place. She did not act crazy like the others—I just could not understand what was transpiring. This was such a sad Christmas for me, one that I shall not forget, with so many mixed emotions and changes in my life.

Later the following year, a new social worker was assigned to work with mother. Mother began to teach her sign language. She discovered mother's physical problem and the reason she was incontinent. The worker informed the attending physician of her discovery and requested a complete physical for mother. The tests revealed that she had a lacerated bladder and that her problem was not mental illness, but she was physically ill.

Surgery was performed and by fall, mother had returned home. Life, by now was so different for all of us. Mother had blamed everyone for the scenario that she had to endure the past few months. Therefore we were often times the recipients of her wrath.

Dad just kept encouraging us and assuring us that she would get better in time. Six months later, she returned to work and appeared to be on the mend. Life was almost back to normal.

The following spring, a new Rockwell Manufacturing Plant opened in Tupelo. Several of the businessmen who were instrumental in helping acquire the industry for the area, assisted Dad in securing employment with the plant. He was hired on as a Lathe Operator. A small man, he had tremendously strong arms and hands. He did very well and was making more money than he ever had in his lifetime.

He purchased us new furniture, acquired a television, purchased a car, (a long Mercury) and I finally had some new shoes from Sears-Roebuck. We were what one would consider in the south, in "High Cotton."

Bubba and I both joined the "Scouts." We were active in all school activities and could finally afford to go to summer camp. Life was going so well for us.

The next few years, we lived a wonderful life. Mother was doing fine. I remained busy, studying and playing the piano. I entered several spelling bees and won several also. I accompanied Mrs. McClanahan to Oxford, Miss. (Ole Miss) for summer seminars in music. These were the years when everything seemed to go so well with us, there were very few problems, and we were the epitome of a happy family. One son, one daughter, with happy parents. We shared many precious moments, even though Mother and Dad could not hear.

One summer, while having our house painted, the painters heard me playing the piano. They were known as the "Scribners," a gospel singing group. Later they asked Mother and Dad if I could accompany them. Their sister was leaving for college shortly and they were in need of a pianist. This was the beginning of my career in learning to play and sing gospel music. We had a radio program and made recordings on Saturdays to be aired on the local radio station each Sunday. In addition, I continued to be active in Bible School at the Methodist Church and to sing in the choir and practice my musical scores on the piano.

Over the years there were numerous people who encouraged me. Of those, Mommie and Aunt Gert always reminded me that I should keep myself in the Lord's will. At the age of twelve, Thurlough Spurr and his brother Theron, came to the Methodist Church for a revival. It was during this revival, that I was saved. I gave my life to do mission work—Mommie always prayed that I would go to "Darkest Africa" where she said the great missionary, David Livingston, needed help. That was my ultimate goal, to do that for my Savior.

At the age of thirteen, a minister in Tupelo, feeling the need of a "Deaf Ministry," in the area, contacted my parents regarding a Revival that was being planned for the local deaf people. Rev. Don Reed of Second Baptist in Tupelo, opened up new avenues for me to begin on my long journey as a "Church Interpreter."

September of 1953, we attended the services, and this was my first experience at observing an interpreter for the deaf. She used hand signals that I had never seen before.

Her nimble fingers raced through the air with the greatest of ease, and each deaf person was in awe of every word said by the minister.

I knew that this must be my calling. I answered the altar call and surrendered my life to this mission. I also joined the Baptist Church at that time. Sunday after Sunday, we sat in the rear of the church with a curtain to protect us from prying eyes, to listen to Rev. Reed expound on the Scriptures, some of which these deaf people in attendance had never heard. I did the best that I could. Later, I was asked to teach the Sunday school class. Since there seemed to be no one in the class who had read the Bible enough to teach it, I usually resorted to acting out Bible Stories that my Mommie had taught me over the years. Dad especially liked the story of Zaccheus, because he could relate to it.

As noted previously, deaf people are very clannish and they enjoy convening on any occasion. The Annual Homecoming at the State School for the Deaf is a big event at any state school. Therefore, whenever there was a meeting of deaf people, they would come for miles around just to have the companionship of another deaf person. This was the case of our Sunday school class in Tupelo. Each Sunday, one of the adult Sunday school classes would provide the lunch for our group. We averaged around thirty members per Sunday. Here was my mission field, and I knew it. Mommie prayed for me with all diligence. She was so proud that there was a church where "Little Carl" could hear/see the Word of God and learn about Jesus and His love. But most of all she was so pleased with me serving the Lord in this way.

My dad was enjoying his work. He kept the Shoe Shop open on Saturdays, and worked at Rockwell during the week. His friends were many and he made new friends everywhere he went.

On my fifteenth birthday, I asked Dad to buy me a pair of pink high heels. Being a shoe man, he said the heels were not good for me because I had flat feet, however, he did resort to purchasing me some wedged heel shoes. They were the brightest pink that you have ever seen. I received them on my birthday as requested, which also happened to be Easter Sunday. I stood in those shoes and interpreted for the deaf one entire hour. The pain was almost unbearable, but I would have never admitted it, because those pink shoes made me feel so much taller than my 4'5".

Dad and Mother were so proud of me. Everywhere I went, they were always boasting of how intelligent I was, and how fortunate I had been in all my accomplishments. Dad especially, petted me, because I was afforded so many opportunities that he had been denied, due only to his deafness. Dad was special. He entertained people. When we went to ball games, he would put his cap on sideways and become the town clown immediately. He knew card tricks, other magical sleight of hand capers, and various monkeyshines to entertain the children, and adults alike. Of course I was delighted with the attention that I derived from his antics.

April of that year, Rockwell, had field day for all of the employees and families. A helicopter ride was on the agenda. Dad, Mother, Bubba and I climbed aboard. That was the highest that I had ever been above the ground. It was a real delight to fly over Tupelo, and Nettleton. We discussed how we felt like birds looking down over the houses and townships. This was an amazing adventure for a deaf couple, and their two teenagers.

Dad also won some of the prizes that were awarded that day. He had made the ashtrays that we passed out as souvenirs. This gave him a real sense of accomplishment. I stood beside him at his machine and interpreted as people would question him regarding his particular task. He stood tall that day, and I shall remember forever the enjoyment we experienced as a family unit at that gathering of people from all walks of life, from the area surrounding North Mississippi. A little deaf man from humble beginnings making it good in the big town at a big machine.

The following week, Dad and Mother went to Tupelo and purchased a new 1954 Ford. It was a perfect car. Unlike the jeep or Mercury, I could even see out of it. This gave me the opportunity to learn to drive, because I had not been able to see out of the big Mercury. At that time, in Mississippi, anyone could secure their drivers license at age fifteen. I immediately wanted my driver's license. Of course, Dad was accommodating, so off to the Mississippi State Patrol Office we went, and now little "Doris Mae," or "Dummy's Little Girl," had grown a little more.

After passing the exam and, arriving back in Nettleton, I drove to all of my friends homes and blew the horn, to let them know that I had "made it." Dad was in the front seat, of course. That night we all went to the skating rink, in Wren, and I was allowed to drive there and back home.

There was a drive-in movie located at Wren, also. I had always wanted to attend one, so Dad, feeling so good, took us to the movie. However, I had to sit on the front seat, with my back to the screen and interpret for Mom and Dad. I could only see the movie reflecting through the back of the window—I never saw "Singing in the Rain" that night, I only heard it.

But my parents were happy and that was the most important thing that I could think of at the moment. I had never been selfish toward them. Always obedient. They were good disciplinarians.

Dad and I were perfect skating partners because we were both short. A good skater, I thoroughly enjoyed rolling the rink with him. Those were good times. "Dummy" and his little girl.

6.
JUNE 14, 1955, MY DAD GOES HOME

My father was an avid fisherman. He loved the water, however, he had never learned to swim. I had a terrific fear of water, caused by a near drowning at the Okolona swimming pool at the age of nine. Dad and Mother were attending a typical "deaf" picnic, and Bubba and I were at the pool. Dad was watching us play around, and little did he realize that my cries were for help. Thinking I was vieing for his attention, he just waved back at me as I struggled to get out of the water. The lifeguard, noticing that something was wrong, darted toward me, but not before a young man had jumped the fence and dragged me from the pool. They administered C.P.R. I shall never forget the feeling of having life pushed back into my body and having the water expelled from my lungs. It was a traumatic experience that I had never overcome. Dad understood my fear of the water. I never wanted him to go fishing alone, so he always took a partner with him. It was usually Bubba or some of his little buddies.

Sunday, June 14, 1955, shall lie in my mind as a day of megrim for the deaf of the state of Mississippi.

The annual "Deaf Picnic" was planned at Sardis Reservoir near Memphis, Tenn. Dad had big plans for that day. Several of his friends had contacted him regarding a week-end fishing trip. Mr. and Mrs. Holmes, an elderly couple who resided in Smithville, Miss., had invited Bubba and Dad to accompany them on Friday, prior to the picnic on Sunday. Their plans were to contact a local commercial fisherman who was deaf and who also resided on the reservoir to take them for a ride. They had planned to ask him to direct them to the good fishing spots on the lake.

Friday came and the Holmes arrived as planned. Dad had worked at Rockwell all day, therefore he was ready for some R. and R. I recall vividly seeing him enter their car—with his Tampa Nugget in his mouth. He waved to me, saying he would see me Sunday. He had bragged that he would catch the largest fish of all, the proverbial dream, to catch the big one.

After their departure, some other deaf friends arrived, and inquired about Dad's whereabouts. One of the young men had just graduated from the school for the deaf, the other had a job and had acquired a new automobile. With pride he showed us his new car.

Mother and I informed them that Dad and the others had left earlier in the day. We signed to them that they were headed for Sardis. The two men said, they, too, were going to Sardis Reservoir and would make a stop in Shannon to locate another deaf friend, a minister's son, to accompany them on the outing. Sunday, plans were to go out on the river early Sunday morning and fish until around ten, then drive over to the picnic by lunch time.

Mother, another deaf friend and I left early Sunday morning for Sardis Lake. About a two hour drive, I was very pleased having been given the responsibility of operating our new auto for that distance.

Arriving at the lake around ten a.m., we were met by several deaf people relating to us that there had been a tragedy, and someone had drowned. The crowd did not know who was involved nor did they have any concrete details to relate to us.

Shortly thereafter the deaf commercial fisherman and his mother arrived on the scene. They were accompanied by another young deaf man, the one who had been by our house earlier on Friday, into the picnic area. There was a quiet hush as it was obvious that the two men were drenched from some sort of water or boating accident. My first reaction was to scream—"Where is Bubba?" In the midst of the crowd, I heard a faint voice reply, "sister, here I am."

Relieved, I waited for the woman to make her announcement. She stated "At approximately seven a.m. this morning, near the 4-H Club campground, three deaf men had drowned. Their names are . . . and Carl Isbell, Sr." I only heard my dad's name called.

I saw my entire life appear before me. I became nauseated, and immediately began to scream. Mother, by my side, fainted. Others around us began to moan and cry. Several members of the crowd gathered to comfort us and to seek medical attention for those of us who were so bereaved. I had never seen Bubba cry. He was always so macho and never seemed to show emotions as I had, however, my little brother, who was now fourteen and developing into a fine young athlete, wept openly.

We were whisked off to the local hospital for medical attention. The police officers and medical staff encouraged us to return home. However, I was adamant and wanted to view the place where my dad had succumbed. Little did I know that the victims' bodies had not been recovered. Rescue operations were now in order and every law enforcement officer, coast guard, experienced boatman, and diver were frantically scanning the choppy waters for possible survivors.

When we arrived on the scene, numerous deaf people had already arrived. The two survivors sat alone on the side of the river bank. The area was very quiet, with the exception of a few audible orders from the law officials. The deaf people were conversing in sign language and hearing people in hushed tones. In disbelief, I surveyed the waters. Surely, my father had swum to the other side and survived. It was all a mistake. He was not in the watery tomb that I was overlooking.

Approximately two hours later, they recovered the body of one of the victims. As I observed them lift his lifeless body from the cold water, I realized it was the man who had the new car. A mournful sound was emitted from the area where the two deaf survivors were waiting. The sound of deaf people in mourning, low guttural and unrecognizable sounds to the natural ear, but one that was audible and understood clearly by one teenager, who had heard them all of her life. One she readily recognized. The deaf in pain.

Thinking the body was that of Dad, I plunged toward the water. However, one of the officials who had been assigned to observe Mother and me, reached to restrain me. Screaming, I wanted to help, I fought like a tiger. The medical officials administered more medication to calm my restless and emotionally encased body.

I ran over to one of the survivors and with fingers flying in the air, words spewed from my hands, I said. "It was all your fault." It was obvious he had been imbibing in alcoholic beverages to the extreme. I was hurt, angry, frustrated, and crushed.

He began to weep. He tried to put his arms around me, however, I would not allow it. I could not permit him to ever do that because Dad had never wanted a deaf man to embrace me. Ever.

My Dad was gone and he could not bring him back. I could not be consoled because of that factor.

Then he reenacted the scene and told me how Dad had held his hand out for help—and his last words were "Take care of Doris Mae." I was "Dummy's Little Girl," until his last breath.

Nettleton seemed like such an empty town when we drove into the downtown area on our way home. Mother, Bubba, a deaf friend and I were so alone in the new automobile. A friend had offered to drive us home following the drowning.

When we rounded the corner of the street, where our little four room house was located, the place we called home, the yard was filled to capacity with people of all ages. The little frame house that Dad and my uncles had built, did not have the significance that it once had. I had never seen so many people in all of my lifetime. They all wanted to know if the stories that had been circulating and being announced on the radio were true. Newsmen stood on the side of the road, microphones in one hand and holding their tape-recorders with the other. It was an awesome sight. I began to weep. Mother placed her arms around Bubba and me as we exited the car. Mommie and Aunt Jean emerged from the crowd. When I spotted Mommie, I could not hold back the anguish that I felt for her. Her first words were "Doris Mae, your little daddy is gone, you and Bubba must be brave for your mother's sake. I'm here to help if you need me."

I knew she would always be there for us. Soon Judy arrived. She took me in her arms and told me that my dad had left many friends and a legacy that would be a memory for a lifetime. She was so comforting to me. Immediately, Aunt Toy went into the house. She, Mrs. Cheek and Aunt Gert began to dust and clean. Preparations were made for all the food that was expected. In addition to the numerous visitors, we would have Dad's body at the house. He would spend his last nights in our little house in Nettleton, known as "Dummy's House."

As expected, the deaf community began to emerge. Phone calls had to be made to all of the relatives at Fellowship. Televisions and radios blared all over the state. " 'Dummy' Isbell of Nettleton, and two companions, drown in Sardis boating accident." The headlines in my beloved Tupelo Journal were similar, the following day. The Jackson Clarion-Ledger, and Memphis Commercial Appeal had recent photographs of all of the victims. Ironically one of the photos was of a group of basketball players from the Mississippi School for the Deaf, picturing all of the victims including the survivors seated on the front row.

As word of the tragedy spread, people came. Some for comfort, some to bring food and others out of curiosity. Over one thousand came on Monday evening to our home. Many of those were Dad's co-workers at Rockwell. Relatives both near and far came. Homes of residents in Nettleton were opened up to accommodate those who had no place to stay. I went home with Judy, that night. I was in such grief but her words were so comforting to me. As we talked into the night, she assured me that everything was going to be all right. I knew they would be, but I just needed the assurance.

There were three funerals to plan. It seemed that every deaf person in the South, had converged on North Mississippi. I did not attend the other two, even though the relatives of the other men came to visit us. Rev. Don Reed was a mainstay to our entire family and the deaf at that time.

Each deaf person who came by, had a variation of the Sunday incident to relate, and of course, the clannishness emerged in all of them. I stood near Dad's casket and stroked the top of his suit. He was the last to be found late Sunday evening around eight p.m. Therefore, his body had become bloated due to the length of time he had remained in the water. He did not depict the strong little man I once knew, and I was not allowed to touch his face. Someone earlier had stated that when his body was recovered the authorities would be able to determine the exact time of drowning, however his Timex watch was still running when he was finally drawn from the murky waters. He lay in the casket with the watch still attached to his arm.

Tuesday evening, prior to the funeral which was scheduled to be held on Wednesday evening, one of the survivors made a call. His request was to be left alone with Dad in the living room. His request was honored and everyone departed the area. Observing from the nearby kitchen, I watched as he stood beside my Dad's casket. Alone, the two of them. I saw him sign to him in the language of the deaf. "You were such a good man, why did God take you and not take me? I will try to be a good man like you and take good care of your family. I promise." My heart melted as I saw this young man, having only graduated from my father and mother's alma mater two weeks earlier, stand there as if he had the entire world on his shoulders. He had immediately lost his popularity among the deaf. Somehow he had felt responsible for the tragedy.

I then entered the living room. I told him that I understood and that no one would hold him responsible. All five of the occupants were adults and took responsibility for their own lives. If they had been drinking, laughing, having a good time and not paying attention, it was their own fault. None of them had bothered to don a life preserver, thinking that nothing could deter their joy in the small home-made craft that was to take them to a watery death.

This tall, young, deaf man placed his arms around me and said he would do his best. He could not promise, since he had always been a playboy and had been irresponsible in many ways. He had always been out for a good time, but this incident had changed his life. He said he had given his life to the Lord on the bank of the river. His young friend who had just drowned the day before, had left a vacancy at the Printing Shop in West Point, and the owner had been at the site on Sunday afternoon. As this young man stood beside my dad's casket, broken-hearted, he related how he had been offered the job of filling the vacancy that the drowning victim had created. At least something good came of this catastrophic incident to the deaf community. He then left, to return to the funeral the following day.

The Rev. Don Reed was to conduct the funeral at the Methodist Church that Dad had learned to love, early in life. Floral arrangements began to pour in from all over the South, some from people that I did not even know existed. The deaf began arriving early on Wednesday. The funeral scheduled for two p.m. would include songs, melodies that my Dad had never heard due to his deafness. Convening at the Methodist Church to our dismay, we discovered there was no interpreter present.

The family members were the last to enter the church auditorium. The Rev. Reed had agreed to read the poem that I had written in honor of my dad. Everything was in order, the choir, the pianist, the deaf seated to one side of the Church, but no interpreter for them. I rose from my seat, stood in front of the deaf congregation gathered to hear the last rites of a beloved friend, prepared to interpret for my Dad's funeral. I looked at Mommie as she said, "Doris Mae, you can do it, your Mother needs you now, so go ahead and interpret for the funeral."

The Choir began their first Hymn, "My Jesus I Love Thee." I completed the song without a tear in my eye. Then, as Rev. Reed stood to read the 23rd Psalm, a young lady entered the church. The funeral directors ushered her to the front, and the daughter of Marion Derrick, a long time friend of Dad's, relieved me and continued to interpret the service for all of my dad and mother's dear deaf friends.

As I took my seat, The Rev. Reed completed the reading then began to read the poem that I had written in memory of Dad. He had always loved my poetry, and this was one that he was now "hearing" for the first time in Heaven, I was sure. Dad had been real special to me and I felt an emptiness like I had never known before.

As I looked around, I remembered the times that he had sat in these very pews, Sunday after Sunday and watched as I sang or played the piano. He would never do that again. I really missed him. Dad was real special and I knew it. His friends knew it also.

He would be missed by many people, but especially by me.

A Deaf Christian's Prayer
by
Doris Mae Isbell

"Do the angels sing in heaven, Lord?
Will I hear music there?
Or must I stand in a corner,
While others join in prayer?
Will I wonder what they are saying, Lord?
Like I often do down here?
Must I sit still and be patient,
While the bells ring loud and clear?

"Can I read your lips in Heaven, Lord?
Or will I be brushed aside?
Will I hide my hands in my pocket,
Because of wounded pride?
Will the saints all stand to praise Thee,
While I in silence wait?
Will there be someone in heaven
To lead me through the gate?

"Do you know Sign Language, Lord?
Will you fully understand
The words that I convey to you
By nimble and swift hands?
Will an angel be there to interpret,
And tell me what You say?
Or will I wait 'til someone points the way?"

And God, who loves the humble,
Whispered into the anxious deaf ear.
"My child has no one told you,
There is no silence here?
Hold out your hands, My little one,
For Heaven all to see.
We've heard them pray so many times,
Each prayer reached up to Me.

"See, all of the angels are waiting,

The gate is open wide.
Your crown of Life is waiting,
And I shall be your Guide.
I have a song to give you.
Your song shall be loud and clear.
Your songs of praise, My dear deaf one
Will be the sweetest song up here."

The funeral ended on a "happy note," as Dad would have it. The entire congregation, including the deaf, were encouraged to sing in Sign Language, "When We All Get To Heaven."

As we filed out of the Methodist Church in Nettleton, the one that my dad had loved so much, I saw many of his longtime friends weeping.

Not only had they lost one of their dearest friends, I had lost the very best pal that I had ever known. He was there one day to encourage me, and the following day, his life had been snuffed out in the twinkling of an eye. I felt so all alone. The loneliness was overwhelming.

The funeral was now over and Dad was buried in the little Shannon town cemetery where several gravesites existed for the Isbell Family. He was the first of Mommie's children to be laid to rest there. The small plot overlooks the small town located between Nettleton and Tupelo. Inscribed on his tombstone was a most appropriate epithet, "To know him was to love him." That was my dad. He was now gone from me.

Riding back home from the cemetery with Uncle Howard and Mommie, I pondered the fate of our little family. Dad was always in control, and I just did not know how we would survive.

Days later, after having written more than 2,000 thank you notes, I walked to town to the shoe shop. He had not left a single shoe unrepaired. I knew that Saturday would arrive and we must dispose of the shoes. Mommie, Mother, Bubba and I gathered on Saturday as usual. His customers all gave their condolences. We had to relive the tragedy repeatedly for the sake of them. I could almost feel Dad's spirit there telling us we needed to sell the shop, that it was no longer useful. It would be so hard, because there were so many memories of him there.

The following Sunday was Father's Day. I awoke with an empty feeling deep inside. I did not want to go to church. This would be the first Sunday in my life that I would wear a white rose to announce that my father was deceased. Fifteen years I had worn the customary red rose on my dress to church.

I gathered some of the flowers that were blooming in the yard. Mother and I agreed that we should go to Tupelo to church, and stop by the cemetery on the way. We drove up to the gravesite. The flowers were beginning to fade. I gathered the wilted ones and placed them in a garbage drum nearby. We placed the mixture of running roses, azaleas, and other garden flowers in an urn on his grave. I left that day, vowing never to return unless it was to bury another family member. We journeyed on to church. During the Sunday school class I informed Rev. Reed that I would and could never interpret nor play the piano again. Shocked at such an announcement, he replied that this would not be what my dad would want from me. I was determined to keep that vow, perhaps I thought it would be a punishment to God for taking my dad from me.

Rev. Reed's sermon was most timely. The young survivor was in the audience. He responded to the altar call as so many other people in attendance that day. Following the service, Rev. Reed called me aside and gently reminded me, that the Lord could just as easily take my talent away as He had given it to me. He also reiterated that if I did not use my hands, that I could easily lose them. Thinking heavily upon what he had said, remembering the day that I was burned, I returned to the evening service and served as the evening pianist. Dad was still alive in my heart and I knew I must be Christ-like to his memory, even on Father's Day. I gave Rev. Don the billfold that I had purchased for Dad several weeks prior to his death. I felt he was the one who deserved it, especially on that day.

Summer came, and it was so very dreary for me at that time. However, I began making friends with Joyce Fowler and Patsy Finley. They could make me laugh when no one else seemed to. Patsy had a brother the same age as Bubba, so we both wound up at the Finley residence often. It was hard spending the summer in such a different way. Mother did not want me to date boys and she was so protective of me. I did not play my piano very much, because each time I would sit down, I could still visualize my dad standing nearby with his hand on the side of the piano so he could feel the vibrations of the music.

Because Mother had been left a widow with teenagers, we were entitled to Social Security benefits. Bubba and I began to receive a small allotment each month. Oft times I would baby-sit for Coach and Jean Carlisle who lived nearby. I had several new dresses custom made for me as clothing had always been a problem because I was so short. Knowing that Dad would be proud, I began to place money in a savings account. I felt his presence all around, and just could not seem to overcome the grief that had been mine.

I visited my Granny Massengill at Fellowship Community for a short time. Returning home, nothing seemed to appease me. The young deaf survivor had begun to come and visit us on Friday afternoons on his way to visit his parents in New Albany. He had a sister, who was in college near West Point, and she would accompany him. We became very good friends, and I loved her dearly, but nothing could take the place of my dad and his encouragement in my life. The young graduate began to attend church on a regular basis. We were fast becoming friends. On Aug. 14, 1955, we were baptized.

It was Mommie's birthday, and she said she could think of no better gift she could receive that day. I had to be careful not to mention the survivor's name because many of my relatives still had strong feelings about him. Not because of his deafness, but they felt he possibly could have helped save Dad from drowning. I did not share their feelings.

Dad's dream for me was to graduate from college, marry a hearing teacher, and have two hearing children to learn sign language. He had a similar dream for Bubba. He wanted him to become a star football player, graduate from high school, win a football scholarship to Mississippi State, graduate from college, marry a hearing woman and have two hearing children to learn sign language. He had often said he did not want us to date or marry a deaf person and be subjected to all the problems he had encountered due to his limitations in life.

I just could not bring myself out of the state of despair that I was in. All summer I felt depressed. I did not want to return to school. Music was not in my bones anymore. I did not want to play for the "Scribners," nor did I want to graduate from High School.

I wanted my dad. I wanted what I could not have. I had a dream, but it could not include my dad.

I was sad most of the time and grieved over his absence.

Dad had always been the driving force in my life. I felt I just could not survive without him. He was gone from me forever. I was never to see his smiling face on this earth again.

One day, I drove to Town Creek, just outside of town. I stood at the end of the bridge and tried to convince myself that I would be much better off if I could just drown like Dad did. However, I recalled someone saying to me that, "Suicide is a permanent solution to a temporary problem." Staring at the water for about an hour, I turned, and went home. Dad would not have wanted this to be one of my dreams.

August was really the time for dog days that year. I could find nothing that made me happy. I had always been chubby, but I began to lose weight. I knew that I was grieving because of Dad. I would visit Mommie often, because she had moved to Aunt Jean's house following Dad's death. Mommie encouraged me to eat more. She felt that it was not good for me healthwise to be so thin. My weight plummeted to eighty-seven pounds. My hair was getting thinner and I knew I must do something fast. But I did not know what to do.

I would talk to the young survivor for hours whenever he came for a visit. He signed so much like Dad and the fact that he was deaf made it more interesting. As I look back, I believe I was looking for a surrogate father.

Uncle Howard was good to me, but he was not like Dad. He would scold me, and Dad never scolded me in a way to make me cry. At fifteen, I had only known my dad a short length of time. He was so young when he died, a mere 47, that I felt I had been deprived of so much.

I could visualize him watching me as I prepared to go to the Junior-Senior Prom, as I walked across the stage of Nettleton High School to receive my diploma. He would never see the joy as I stood proudly to receive my scholarship, to attend the Concerts that I would enter at Ole Miss, to see me graduate from that stately old school; to escort me down the aisle of

Nettleton Methodist Church and give me away to a tall handsome hearing man in a beautiful wedding; to hear him laugh with joy when he saw his first grandson; to take the little tyke fishing and show him all the magical tricks he always held up his sleeve. I could just see him teaching him how to ride a motor scooter, as he did Bubba and me. The picture so vivid in my mind would be that he would make an apple box car with a steering wheel attached that when one turned it to the left the box would turn right. In the corridors of my mind that summer, I felt I had been deprived of seeing my dad retire and receive a new watch with a Rockwell logo, with his name inscribed on it. I could still feel the music of the jukebox as we would skate around the rink together at Wren. My children, his grandchildren, would never know the talents he possessed. They would never hear his laugh—even though it sounded like a billy goat. They would never stand beside him when they reached ten years of age to measure his stature, to see if they were taller than Grandpa. Oh! How I missed him and what he had meant to me over the years.

The deaf survivor more or less filled that void. He was talented and had so many of the mannerisms that Dad possessed. However, he was a tall athletic kind of person. He loved to swim, fish, hunt, fool around with cars and the like. A personable man, he respected me and my strong faith in God. He knew that I was a prayer warrior. He also knew I was lonely and missed my father and his companionship.

In September of 1955, I entered the tenth grade at Nettleton High School. I had no desire to attend school. I did however volunteer to be the scorekeeper for the basketball team, a job that I had retained since the eighth grade. Bubba was now playing football.

He was aiming for his dream. I could not muster up any dreams. School was boring. My energy was at an all time low. I did not have the interest in boys that I had the previous year. All I could think about was getting away. Running away from everything. I did not know where I wanted to run to, but it sure was not to Nettleton. I talked to Mommie a great deal on the telephone. We had been able to afford one, since I was now receiving the small amount of money each month. Mommie tried to encourage me, but to no avail. She told me I needed to talk to Rev. Reed. I spent some time with the Reeds, but they had five daughters younger than I, and I felt they just did not know the magnitude of my emotional problem concerning the loss of my dad.

I tried to get involved in the church in Tupelo, which would take me out of Nettleton and all of my memories. I met some nice people there, but there was still the void.

One afternoon, I drove over to Uncle Howard's, and asked if I could just move in with them. They had two daughters who had already completed college, and one young son a year younger than I, remaining at home. He discouraged the idea because he was afraid that it would cause Mother to become emotionally upset or become angry with him. For Dad's sake, he did not want to take on this responsibility.

I was in a dilemma. I began to write letters to some deaf boys at the Mississippi School for the Deaf. Unsure, but possibly I did this out of rebellion. I would have them send their return mail to Judy or Patsy's address. The survivor's address was the one that I sent the most mail to. During that time he was residing with one of the victim's parents. He loved them, and they loved him. Their youngest son, was also deaf and still a student at the school. The young survivor was happy at what he was doing, but he knew how very unhappy I was. Sensing that something was terribly wrong, he would try to spend as much time alone with me as possible, however Mother would not allow this. She would want to accompany us everywhere we went, therefore our means of communication was limited to conversing in her presence. The only secrets that we had were through writing to each other.

October came and my depressed feelings accelerated. I felt a real need to leave home. The memories were too much. I could not eat, nor could I sleep. I dreamed of Dad all the time and how much I missed him.

The hedges in the front yard had been cut down that summer by some accommodating young men at Mother's request. Resenting the fact since Dad had planted those, my feelings became very negative toward Mother.

She was tightening the noose around my neck. We could not agree on anything. Bubba kept his distance. He never worried about anything, just football and girls. I did most of the cooking and cleaning, just out of sheer boredom.

Halloween came, and I wanted to attend the Carnival, but Mother would not allow me to go to the festivities alone. The resentment was increasing. I had no privacy and it seemed all we ever did was fuss or argue.

November 6, 1955 was the anniversary for the Second Baptist Church in Tupelo, Mississippi. All of the deaf attended the reunion. There was a big cake provided from the bakery. The young survivor was in attendance as usual with his sister. As on previous occasions, we had much to talk about as it seemed that we had so much in common. She was two years older than I, but felt more like a sister than a friend.

Following the activities of the day, the young survivor said that he would come by our house for a visit after he took his sister home. Sunday afternoon was a time of gathering at the Dairy Queen in Nettleton. Prior to Dad's death, I enjoyed going there to get ice cream. After Dad passed on, I did not find it interesting anymore. I had plans and I was determined to complete them this time. Leaving home was foremost in my mind. I did not know how I would accomplish it, as I had no accomplice, but I was determined. Around seven, I asked Mother if she and Bubba would like for me to bring them some ice cream from the Dairy Queen. They gathered up the extra change they could find, and I went to my bank to get all of the eighty dollars that I had been saving for this time. I left, rode past the Dairy Queen and onto Highway 45. I did not stop, nor did I have any real destination in mind.

Time began to pass. I drove through Shannon, past the cemetery. Looking toward Uncle Howard's house, I continued to drive. At Shannon, I turned left to go toward Okolona, or West Point, or possibly to Fellowship to Granny's. Granny's place was a four hour drive and I knew it.

In Okolona, I stopped at a gas station to purchase some gasoline and drinks. I did not know how long it would be before Mother would have the State Patrol searching for me. I continued to drive. Around midnight, I became very sleepy. I pulled to the side of the road, and fell asleep. Resuming my trip, I knew that I was nearing the Prairie area, where the Army Depot was located. Becoming frightened that perhaps some military personnel would find me, I drove into the parking area of the local church and fell asleep again.

Around two, I began to drive down the highway again, very slowly, so as not to fall asleep. I noticed a vehicle behind me. The lights were on bright. They began to flicker. Immediately my thoughts were that Mother had summoned the Patrol, and I would be taken to jail as a runaway. I, being the obedient person that Mommie and Dad had taught me to be, pulled onto the edge of the highway. To my great surprise, it was the deaf survivor. He was astonished to see me. He then instructed me to pull into the parking area of a local store and we would talk. He had an older car, and felt he could leave it there while we went somewhere to talk. I did not want to leave with him alone, at 2:00 in the morning. Being frightened, I told him so. He told me not to worry, that he would take good care of me. Somehow I trusted him. He had promised my dad he would do that. He, like Dad, was someone I thought I could trust with my life.

We then discussed the problems that I was having at home. I told him that I would not return, but I did not know where I would go. He stated that he felt an obligation to me because of Dad, therefore he would marry me and take care of me. He did say that he felt like we were sister and brother, and that he did not love me romantically.

At that point in time, I did not care. It was an escape route. We then went to West Point, informed his boss that he would be absent from work the following day. He also informed his friend's mother and picked out a suit to wear to our wedding.

Driving back through Okolona, we stopped to call Mother and Bubba to inform them that I was okay. Bubba called me crazy and a couple of other expletives. Mother stated that she knew that the young man and I had been seeing each other secretly for quite some time, which was untrue. I had never been with him alone.

The following day, November of 1955, the young deaf survivor and Doris Mae Isbell, daughter of Florence Massengill Isbell and the late Carl Morehead Isbell, Sr. of Nettleton, Mississippi were united in wedlock in a home ceremony at the Second Baptist Church Pastorium in Tupelo, Mississippi. The Rev. Don Reed performed the double ring ceremony with Mrs. Florence Isbell and Mrs. Reed present. The couple will reside in

West Point, Miss., where he is employed at a Printing Co. The announcement shocked the entire deaf community, the Isbell and Massengill clan, all of Nettleton, and Tupelo. I was happy I now had a home of my own, and a husband that would take care of me.

7.
ANOTHER DEAF MAN ENTERS MY LIFE

At fifteen, I knew very little about being a wife, much less being a house-wife. I was too young to get a job, so I did the best I could at trying to be a doting housewife. Our little three room apartment was adjacent to the City Library. I spent much of my time there during the week, reading and gathering all the information that I could on any subject nameable. I desired to return to school, but felt it would be impossible at this stage, in a new town, and a new place.

February came, and through the assistance of my husband's boss, I began work as a Nurse's Aide at the local hospital. I enjoyed my work. Late in April, following my sixteenth birthday, I discovered that I was pregnant. Mommie came to visit us often. I enjoyed her visits, because she would teach me little tricks about housekeeping, sewing, etc. Mother came to visit some, whenever Bubba would drive her down. They helped us out tremendously, especially financially.

August, I left my employment at the hospital. My husband had wanted to move to a larger apartment, downtown, directly above the pool hall. He could not hear the noise, but it almost ran me crazy, being pregnant and summer did not make for a good combination.

My cousin Hal and his wife Ann (Aunt Jean's son), who resided in West Point, lived in a very comfortable apartment in a nice section of town. They were planning to move, therefore it was an excellent time for us to move to plan for the arrival of the new baby. Mom Fulgham, another surrogate, lived next door.

Mommie was not happy when she learned of my pregnancy. She felt I was too young to be a mother, and with the complications that I had experienced over the years, she was confident that I would have problems both carrying and delivering a baby.

Being 4'5" was not to my advantage. Ironically the physician that I chose to assist me, was the same doctor who had botched Mother's surgical procedure. I did not have a choice, since Mother's insurance covered my care if I had the baby in Tupelo, rather than in West Point.

I gained weight rapidly. I looked like a walking butterball. Mommie was so concerned about my health, she spent a lot of time with me. She had planned to stay with me following the birth, but at 79, she chose not to be with me during the birth of the baby.

My doctor had informed me that if I gained too much weight that the baby would be too large, and it would endanger my health. I made efforts to try to curtail the weight gain, but they were unsuccessful.

Winter came and the date of arrival was nearing. It was difficult for me to breathe, much less sleep. I was having numerous problems, especially with edema in my feet. The doctor decided to admit me to the hospital. He placed me on a restricted diet and had me walking the stairs day and night. Mommie was concerned also that the baby might be deaf, since mother had so many deaf relatives, the possibilities were extremely high. I was not concerned, I just wanted the baby to be healthy. Hearing or deaf, it didn't matter.

Uncle Howard visited me daily in the hospital, then would call Mommie and give her an update on my condition. I thought of Dad. The Fulghams and Mildred called daily.

At five o'clock, on the fifth day of my hospital stay, Uncle Howard paid a visit. While he was there I informed him that I needed help, that was when we discovered that the baby was on its way. I was rushed off to the labor room. I remained in the labor room for two hours, making no progress. The nurses and others began to coach me. I knew that Mommie was praying. The doctor came in and said the baby was in distress and that they would have to perform a C-section. I prayed earnestly that the baby would come naturally, because I did not want to be botched like Mother. While they were preparing the operating room, the baby decided to come.

Entering into our lives now was the most beautiful baby that

I had ever seen. This was my love child. This was the first thing that I could truly say was my very own. I truly loved him. But I gave him to the Lord for His keeping too.

A week later we went home and Mommie was there to help me and my deaf husband with the baby. She would lay her hands on the baby and pray for him each day. She would say, this is going to be my preacher boy.

I tried very hard to be a good mother. Mommie taught me many things about mothering and bonding as it was obvious that she had a great deal of experience. She told me to start teaching him immediately. Even though he was a tiny baby she said, that if I would sing to him, and talk to him, he would learn much faster. He did learn, quickly. Just like she said. God had blessed me with a healthy child. Not deaf, nor deformed, but intelligent and pretty.

I thought many times how my dad would have enjoyed playing with his first grandbaby. I could visualize him acting like a clown and putting his cap on side-ways, crying like a baby and dancing around the room. I could picture him teaching him to throw a football and playing with him in the yard or the swing set. There were many pictures vivid in my mind that my dad would have enjoyed doing with my firstborn. Mother saw us often, we referred to her as "Mama Flo."

Our firstborn was always friendly. He never seemed to meet a stranger anywhere. Most important to me, he loved music. I noticed that he possibly might have inherited some of my musical abilities. He loved Mom Fulgham too.

My piano was still at Mother's. I would play it for the baby every chance I had when we visited her.

I did not have a radio, nor did I have a piano, so it was my responsibility to make the music in the house. Each day as I prepared meals or cared for the baby, I would sing, hum or tell the baby fairy tales. Like Mommie, I would teach him other things that were educational, and would assist him in the learning process.

He was very bright and although I did not have the professional knowledge to determine at that time, it appeared to me that he had a photographic memory.

As time progressed, my homemaking skills improved and I began to feel better about myself and my little family. I did so want to be a good mother, wife, housewife and good Christian. That was the ultimate goal in my life. I felt that I was on the road to fulfilling at least some of my dreams. Dad would have been proud that I could make a banana pudding.

In early '58, I discovered that I was once again pregnant. I was very happy, because by this time, I had begun working at the local garment factory as a machine operator. Rosie, our maid, was wonderful with our first born. She loved him like a mother, and he loved her, too. I could leave him with her, never worrying one minute about leaving him in her care.

Into my second pregnancy I was not doing well at all physically and began to have black-out spells at work. Realizing that I might possibly endanger the baby I finally had to give up my job. Rosie came once a week, while I did the shopping.

As time progressed, I knew this was an unusual pregnancy, unlike the first one. I felt confident that this baby would be a little girl, as I had gained so little weight.

The doctor in West Point informed me that I should not plan to have other children, since I was having such a difficult time. I had edema so very badly in my legs that I was unable to walk. The summer heat and lifting the other baby did not help at all. I broke two ribs one day while trying to place him in his crib. This made the pregnancy even more painful.

I was determined, regardless of the obstacles. Mommie would be there to help and I could rely on her. If it had not been for her reassurance, I do not think I would have made it through.

Well into the sixth month, I did not even appear as if I were pregnant. My legs were swelling. I began to experience severe headaches. Not wanting to be a burden, I would not inform the doctor.

In the fall I began to experience terrible headaches that would not ease, no matter what remedy I tried. The doctor had highly recommended that I enter the hospital immediately as there was evidence of toxemia and an impending stroke.

Following a hurried admission, they began to induce labor. They were experiencing difficulty because my blood pressure was well over 200 and I felt that my head would burst wide open.

I remained in the hospital from Monday until Friday. Early Friday morning the attending physician informed us that if the baby did not arrive by evening they would be compelled to operate. As with the previous birth, I began to pray. I knew Mommie was praying for she had come to attend to the other baby. I talked with her daily and she would lift my name in prayer.

At 5:00 p.m. on Halloween, Friday, an autumn day in 1958, John Carl was born. Such a tiny baby, he looked like a little drowned rat when the nurse showed him to me for the first time. Weighing in at 3 lbs. 11 oz. He was 15" long. It was ironic that he was so much different than the older one. Again, I thought of Dad. John-John as we called him was Dad's namesake. We also chose the name John, to honor other family members. John-John was a little doll, but he cried. Oh! how he cried. He would not sleep, he could not eat and had difficulty in swallowing. When he weighed 5 pounds, we took him home, to cry some more.

The doctor was concerned, because he continued to lose weight and could not retain any food. He was considered a failure to thrive baby. We were all so concerned. On my knees one night, I asked for divine guidance.

I tried a goat's milk formula, breast milk, and everything nameable. Finally, Mommie suggested that we try diluted homogenized milk. Surprisingly enough, it worked. John-John was eight months old by that time. I can recall getting my first full night's rest following his bedtime feeding of "Barber's Milk."

John-John began to gain weight. He loved his daddy and "brubber." They both enjoyed going to the farm with their daddy and visiting with their other grandparents.

Prior to John-John's first birthday, his other grandmother died. It was a great loss, but I did not grieve this time as before. She was in God's hands and did not suffer anymore.

Sunday mornings found us going to church faithfully in Tupelo. We were considered "Tent Makers." The pastor had been instrumental in establishing a new church in a residential area of Tupelo. We felt we were being useful to the deaf in the area.

The church had an active deaf ministry. We would arise early on Sunday morning, make our rounds through the countryside between West Point and Tupelo. Any deaf person who did not have a ride, could accompany us to church.

The deaf in the North Mississippi area would travel for miles around to attend the services. It was an all day affair. Sunday school services in the morning, church being interpreted by me, lunch, then afternoon church services for the deaf.

8.
MY MOMMIE GOES HOME

It was early August of 1960. The telephone rang and Uncle Howard was on the other end of the line. His voice had a different tone, therefore I knew something definitely was wrong.

His statement was that Mommie was in the hospital in Amory and they wanted us to come immediately.

I was all involved in moving, but called to the Print Shop to inform my husband immediately. He offered to take the children to New Albany to his aunt's house, and come by and pick up Mother, in Nettleton. I then drove on to Amory to see Mommie in the hospital.

Mommie had suffered a massive heart attack earlier in the day, but she had survived. She was in the Coronary Care Unit encased within an oxygen tent. I did not recognize her, because I had never seen her without her dentures. She looked so old with her hair down and at 82. I always thought she would live forever.

She talked to us with a strained voice. She said that she was going to Heaven. Her work here on earth was over and I was a big girl now, that I had someone to care for me even though he was deaf. I tried not to cry. Earlier I had told her we were planning to go to a Christian College. Questioning about our move, she wanted to know all of the details. I tried to tell her the best I could, but my heart was not in it. I knew that her time was short. The doctor said that the only reason that she was alive was because of her determination and stamina to see all of her children and grandchildren before she succumbed.

I drove to Aunt Jean's house, where Mother joined me later. We made numerous efforts to locate Bubba in south Alabama where he had gone with some friends on a fishing trip. Later we learned that the message had been misunderstood, and another friend came home instead of Bubba. Therefore, Bubba did not arrive as expected. Aunt Katie King was now residing in Bloomington, Texas. We knew that it would be early the following morning before she arrived, however we prayed that Mommie would hang on.

Aunt Katie arrived with Uncle Otha around 2:00 a.m. Mommie had been semi-conscious, but she revived enough to recognize her, and talk with her. The following morning, we went to see Mommie again. She was still in a semi-conscious state, but revived enough to hold her hands up and say "Glory Hallelujah, I'm finally going home." She said the angels were waiting with open arms, she could see little Carl and Joseph waiting on the other side. She talked of her beautiful mansion. She had told everyone who entered the room about the beautiful streets of gold. The beauty, she said, she could not describe to us, only that we should not miss any of it. She told us that she had prayed to go quickly and not linger, and the Lord had answered her prayer. Then she closed her eyes to never open them again.

Around two that afternoon, Mommie entered Heaven in the arms of Jesus. Her prayers had been answered. All of them. Mommie was special. Dad was special, just like her.

Shannon Methodist Church held all of her relatives as she had requested for her funeral. "Beautiful Isle of Somewhere," rang out in tones that I had never heard before. Mommie was now in Heaven. She was laid to rest, beside Dad in Shannon cemetery.

I did not grieve for Mommie like I had for Dad. This time, I had been given the opportunity to say good-bye.

She had lived a long life, and had seen some of my dreams materialize. I knew she was at rest and happy. I loved her. I would miss her too. She had not only been my grandmother, she had been my first teacher, often my only nurse, a mentor, and someone to encourage me everyday of the year.

She was the one who instilled in me an interest in music. She, too, was the one who was always there and had told me that I was special and would have a long and happy life. Mommie wanted the best for all of her children, but I had the innate feeling, that she wanted the very best for me also.

Mommie had been such a great help to me over the years. I

was now 18 and had known her only three more years than I had known my own father. Two of my very, very best friends were now gone to Heaven. However, I did not have too much time to grieve. I had a deaf husband, and two little boys to care for. We had a mission to accomplish, that was to minister to the deaf in the United States. Mommie would have been proud of me. Dad would have too. I felt somehow that Mommie was filling him in on all that had transpired with "Dummy's Little Girl," during her first day in Heaven. She would be able to converse with him now, she no longer needed to use her fingers. No longer would my dad be deaf, because they were in Heaven.

OF MOMMIE
by
Doris Isbell Crowe

She was a mighty woman,
One that was fair of face.
Who taught each little child of hers
To give praise and say his grace.

Her hands they were so nimble,
Could stitch and sew till done.
Then cook a most delicious meal
That all knew was second to none.

Her faith would never waiver
When on her, the kids could call.
Always ready and so willing
She stood ready to help us all.

As her hair turned to different colors,
From black, to shades of gray,
We knew that she was getting older
And some day would go away.

To a land she often spoke of
Away beyond the blue,
A place that held no "hand me downs,"

Where everything was new.

My Mommie left some memories
That will never go away.
I shall ne'er forget her training
Until my dying day.

She sure was one great warrior,
One that prayed to God above.
And nursed each of her loved ones
With kindness, joy and love.

My Mommie'll never really know
Till I reach the Great Divide,
That had it not been for her,
I probably would have died.

9.
THE FIRST TEN YEARS (BABIES)

I knew that another chapter had ended in my life. Soon we would be travelling three hundred miles away from the security of home. I would no longer have Mommie or Dad to rely on. It was a time of change for all four of our little brood.

One of my concerns was for Mother. This was a real problem. Bubba had graduated from high school two years previously, and fulfilled one of my dad's dreams for him. He had won a scholarship to Memphis State, and was now playing football there. The fall would take him away from home, and Mother would have no one to check on her each weekend as I had always done.

Upon arriving back at our hometown, our house was in disarray. We were living in the trailer, and disposing of things from the house. I made a phone call to the Superintendent of the State School for the Deaf. I inquired if there were any openings, and possibilities of employment for Mother at the school. If she could secure employment there, she would be among the deaf, and have the security that she needed. He stated that he did indeed have an opening, and would be delighted to have her on his staff.

So the little "Shoe Shop" in Nettleton and Mother's house were sold. She disposed of all the things that Dad and she had collected over the years. Some of the things were stored in Uncle Howard's garage for Bubba in case he needed them at a later date. My beloved piano was given to a church in Tupelo.

I had no more ties to Nettleton, other than Judy. Judy had married and was working with her dad in his business. She seemed to be very happy. I called her at intervals, but I knew that when we arrived in Tennessee, that there was the possibility that it might be some time before we would see each other again.

We drove through Nettleton once more, just to visit Aunt Gert. Uncle Pipe had died the year before, and she was still living at the old home place. I always enjoyed my visits with her. We passed the Shoe Shop and our little house. There were so many memories there that I began to cry. I was now 20, and the tree that Dad had planted in our yard when I was five had grown considerably. Some trees grow tall, some grow small, this was a tall tree. Much taller than I by now.

Our home of five years, since our marriage, loomed in the distance. There were many memories there also. We had lived in four different locations during the years we lived there. We had friends all over town.

Arriving home, there was much work to be done. We had only one week to complete our move then leave for college. School would begin in three weeks. We had mixed emotions, but were confident that we would make it.

We built a bunk bed outfit in the trailer to accommodate both of the boys, they liked their new home even though it was crowded.

The children had made numerous friends during our stay in this town. They hated to leave their good friends, but we knew they would make new ones wherever we went. With strong feelings but knowing that we must follow God's will, we reluctantly let it all go.

Judy
by
Doris Isbell Crowe

When we were small and not so tall
We shared so many dreams.
Still o'er the years, we've been good friends
Forever, it does seem.

I still recall that Christmas Eve
When with your mom you called,
And brought this little friend of yours,
A gift, the best of all.

As time raced on, you went your way
To make your life complete.
You too, like me, went through a time
When you felt so much defeat.

But you, like me, did persevere
And made it through it all.
You'd not give up, nor even give in
Until the Lord did call.

And now as we are growing old
Our memories still remain.
Of that little town, where we grew up,
And knew everybody's name.

 The day of moving came. We closed our bank account, taking every bit of the money that we owned in the world with us. Neighbors came to wish us well, and tears were shed.
 Mother had already moved to her new home, so our farewells had been made to her. Bubba was now in football practice in Memphis, so we were rather alone when we left.
 Highway 45 seemed so straight and forward as our 1955 Chevrolet automobile pulled the thirty-eight-foot trailer toward the distant city. We had never pulled a trailer before. We knew nothing about hitches, equalizers, and the other jargon affiliated with trailers. Our mobile home was to be our home

for four years, and it was necessary to take great care that we did not damage it in the move.

We stopped several times on the way. The children had never seen the Tennessee River, Lookout Mountain or other sights on our route. They were in awe. We were scared, but we were acting on our faith.

We arrived late at night at the trailer park where we had planned to park the mobile home. It was near another couple who could communicate with us. They had a deaf son, so we had some companionship, when we were not in school.

Looking diligently for work, we were turned down by every place that we sought employment. It was a difficult time for deaf people to find employment. As the days went by, we began to live from hand to mouth. I never thought we would resort to accepting food from the "Food Pantry," and leftovers from the kitchen at the school. But we did, gladly, in order to feed our family.

School began for us. Classes were much different than they had been at the school for the deaf. Much of my time was spent in the library reading required material for our classes, then explaining to my deaf husband what I had read. I served as his interpreter in the morning classes, then in the afternoon I worked in the school nursery to pay for our school bill and nursery care for the children. We were happy even though we were poor. We relied heavily on our faith and on the Lord for our support.

The president of the school met us one day after noticing that we seemed to be having some problems. He gave us some money allocated as a benevolent fund for needy students. It certainly did aid in getting us by for another month.

We were acquiring more than a college education. We were learning about faith and experiencing life without depending on others. We were without the security of the School for the Deaf as we had been accustomed. And I did not have the security of Mommie and Dad as I once had. We just had each other, our little family, and the Lord. That was the most important aspect, that the Lord was on our side.

Later the president of the college, asked if we were interested in becoming the janitors for the chapel. Our days were busy. Each morning, I would interpret for him, take a tape recorder to school, work in the nursery in the afternoon, then take notes from the recorder at night. When we had to clean the chapel, we would do it as a team, even the boys learned how to dust. We made it through the year with few problems. The following summer we attended a local Christian ranch. Moving the mobile home to the ranch, was quite a task. We enjoyed the summer there and learned much about mission work and dealing with the deaf from all walks of life.

In the fall of 1961, the daughter of a famous evangelist, entered school with us. I served as her interpreter, and was paid a salary to do so. So therefore we were doing much better financially.

We were accepting invitations to speak at various churches. We were featured in the Bill Rice Magazine, and also the New York Times. People were beginning to recognize us wherever we went.

We accepted the position of ministering to the people in a neighboring state once a month. Driving down on Friday afternoons, we would visit all day Saturday, then conduct services on Sunday. Following the services in the afternoon, we would begin our trek back to Chattanooga with two little sleepy headed boys in the backseat.

My husband finally landed a full-time job. Attending school in the mornings, he would leave school, then go to the job site in a neighboring town. Arriving home late in the evening, it was noticeable that he was tiring easily now. He felt that he should drop out of school for a quarter. I really did not want him to do this, but knew he must do so for health reasons.

In the spring of 1963, we were offered the part-time missionary position at a large Baptist church in the south. I was now working at a dress factory in the city. My husband had returned to school and now had another person in his class who could interpret for him. We were doing well financially. He was the house-husband while I worked.

I began to have dizzy spells and problems with my back. Attributing it to the long hours at the sewing machine, I overlooked it. The pain continued for weeks, and becoming more concerned, I finally went to the doctor, and much to my surprise, discovered that I was now pregnant again.

With joy, I announced to everyone that we were to have a

new addition to our family. The back problems persisted, as the scoliosis in my back was being aggravated by the weight. I was required to wear a brace to keep my back straight andd hold up my stomach.

The baby was due in the fall. We continued to serve as missionaries at the church in the south. The deaf congregation were very concerned, because I was required to stand on a stool in order for them to see me as I interpreted for the minister. Due to that fact, and obviously being very much pregnant, I had the undivided attention of everyone present.

This pregnancy, I felt was going much different than the other two. I was 23 and had enough experience to know when I had taxed my body to the limit. With the other doctor's words ringing in my ears that we should not have any more children, I was not going to take any chances this time. I wanted a girl. That was the only thing on my mind.

The city where the college was located, was a unique place. The college was even more unique than the town. However, it was home to us, at the present.

We learned some hard lessons about depending on the Lord for substance while we lived there and went to school. The idea of running to relatives, to the bank, or even asking a neighbor to borrow a couple of dollars, never entered our minds.

My husband had to resort to pawning his prized gun to purchase gas for us to drive our automobile. By now we had given up the new Chevy and were driving an old Plymouth. It did not look like much, but at least it was serviceable.

I felt that since my children's dad had relinquished one of his prized possessions, that I should be able to do likewise. I sold my ring that Judy had given to me. It was the only possession that I had that was worth any money. My deaf girlfriend had admired it for quite some time and since she could afford it financially, and realizing the need, she paid a nice price for it. Pangs of grief went through my heart as I turned my coveted piece of jewelry over to her care.

I cried softly before going to sleep that night. I did not want the boys to hear me, nor to know how much that ring had meant to me. My husband never heard my cries. The only way that he ever knew that I had cried, was by feeling my face on the wet pillow by his side.

Hiding my disappointment, I knew my family was far more important than a sentimental ring that I had received as a child. Furthermore, at that time, we needed food. I trusted the Lord and His goodness. There were better days ahead I knew.

Our dear deaf friend, and our little family were facing the holidays. In order for our family to have a decent meal we spent Thanksgiving at a Gospel mission in the ghetto part of town that year. Our dinner, with all the trimmings were shared with the homeless at that large city and surrounding areas. It was a most humbling experience that we shall never forget.

Because of that experience, until this day, we recall that year and tell the story at Thanksgiving to remind us of where we have been and how far we have come.

Following the meal, the director's wife took us upstairs to the clothing closet. We chose numerous clothing for each member of the family. Somewhere in that large city, a short woman, who was my exact height and weight had donated a coat to the mission. I was the recipient of that coat. I took it home and thanked the Lord for all His goodness in caring for me and for my little family.

I had always taught my children that although we were poor we should never be dirty nor dressed with clothing that was not clean. The trip to the mission certainly made my life easier that year.

The boys were all involved in their nursery school. Both of them had learned Bible verses and had been asked to quote scriptures in their presentation at the large church we attended. Each was given a little Bible tie tack for his performance. At the tender age of four and two, this reminded me of days gone by, when I had made my parents so proud of me. Now my boys were performing, and their words too, were falling on deaf ears, their dad's.

Christmas came. We knew that we had no money whatsoever to purchase the children any toys. I gently told the boys that it was Jesus' birthday, and we had no gifts to give them, but give Him thanks for a roof over our head and shoes on our feet. We all had a good bed apiece and plenty of food to eat. But that was all. No money.

The neighbors knowing our plight would not allow two little

boys to go without some sort of gift at Christmas. Upon returning from the church Christmas party, where they had received fruit and warm caps each, we realized that we had failed to lock the door.

As we carefully opened the door, not knowing what to expect inside, to our utter surprise, there were toys all over the room. Our deaf girlfriend, having been made aware of the plan, had insisted on accompanying us home that evening.

The boys squealed with delight at the gifts, each one, exactly what they had requested. The look on their faces was one never to be forgotten.

Our friend had a small gift for us. We had nothing to give her, but our love. My husband opened his present to discover that the pawn ticket had been paid for his gun. He was now able to retrieve it. As I opened my gift last, I knew that it must be something special. Lying in the middle of the soft cushioned "Sears" gift box was my ring that Judy had given to me so many, many years ago. I could not hold back the tears, nor the joy at such a delightful gift. This ring had thrilled "Dummy's Little Girl," once again.

We were poor, but the Lord had blessed us with good friends and met our needs. This time He had supplied our wants too.

We were all excited about a new addition to the family. I, of course, was praying for a girl. The others didn't seem to care. Names had been carefully chosen by everyone. Some very humorous. Others outlandish. One thought we should name a boy Mickey Mouse, and if the baby happened to be a girl she should be named Plymouth (after our car). My husband's sister had agreed to come and help me when the baby came. She knew the problems that had existed during the other two pregnancies, and she also knew Mommie was no longer around. I could feel her spirit and somehow I knew that her prayers were for me. I did not think of Dad as much these days except when one of my boys, his namesake, acted like him.

Bubba had completed his college education, and had married a young lady, in a beautiful wedding ceremony. Dad's dreams for him had been fulfilled. I had not accomplished the first dream that Dad had for me, but I still felt I was in the Lord's will. Serving Him as an interpreter for the deaf in churches.

Early one morning found me awake with an uneasy feeling. It was approximately 4:00 a.m.

I woke my husband and informed him that I thought the baby was on the way. Since this was my third child, and I had been in perfect health with no complications, edema, or headaches, I was expecting an easy birth. I was twenty-three at the time. However I was not going to take any chances.

My husband woke the children and took them to the next door neighbor to keep, until he could take them to the nursery later in the morning. He was still in school, and a test was planned for that day. The rules were strict and absences were frowned upon.

We then journeyed to the hospital. My mate then left around eight after the doctor informed him that I would probably be in labor for about eight more hours. He returned at nine thirty to check on me. Knowing that the birth was imminent I informed the nurses to have him wait. Not understanding what they were telling him, I was required to write him a note myself. Even though I was in great pain, I wanted my husband to wait. The doctor assured me that the baby would not come until late afternoon, I knew better. The attending physician left for his office, and sure enough the baby came. I called for a nurse to assist me, ultimately the nurse and I delivered our third son. This was the first experience that I had ever had at natural childbirth. I felt great, and he was a real doll.

His dad was very excited, and could not believe it when he saw me so well and alert. He left immediately to get his sister and bring her to help me with the children.

The baby was such a perfect baby. He favored the others, and fortunately he was not branded with any of the odd names that had been previously chosen by the little brood at home.

We now had three boys, and I felt certain that I must settle for having granddaughters. The doctor again recommended that I not have any more children. This was not one of my dreams. I wanted a little girl so badly.

Regardless, I thanked the Lord for His goodness in helping me through the past eight years, and blessing us with this little angel.

The new addition added much to our lives that winter. He was such a sweet child. We had decided once again that I would support the family, and the children would stay at home with their dad. My husband would become a house-husband once again.

Early in the spring, our new son became gravely ill. He was teething at the time, and could not retain even the mildest of foods in his stomach. He never cried much, but we knew that he was very sick. I called the pediatrician and related to him my concern about the baby. Hours later his temperature began to rise. We took him to the hospital in the large city to be told that they could not help there. We then transported him to the smaller hospital in the county in which we lived. Enroute, the baby had a convulsion. I was petrified. I thought surely my baby would die in my arms.

When we finally arrived at the hospital, an Oriental female intern whisked him away before I could say anything. Here I stood in the corridor of the hospital—facing a deaf husband and the possibility of a dead child inside the emergency room. How my heart ached for someone like Mommie or Dad to be nearby to help ease my pain.

We began to pray. I called our pastor, and related our problem. He said that he would ask others to pray also. Our little one was placed in the Intensive Care Unit and we were later allowed in to see him. He was unconscious and had tubes, wires and needles in his lifeless little body. It was unbelievable, that just the previous day our seven month old little angel had been laughing and crawling around the mobile home.

I prayed like I had never prayed before. My husband wept openly because he felt that the Lord was trying to tell us something. We were also concerned because we had no insurance and no funds whatsoever to pay for the expenses that were being incurred due to this child's hospitalization. I felt assured that the Lord would take care of it. I trusted Him. I always trusted my husband also, when he said things like trusting in the Lord with all of our heart.

For five days, our son lay lifeless in the hospital. I slept on the couch and refused to leave. On the fifth day, the nurses insisted that I leave, go home and take a shower, change clothing and get some much needed rest.

I did go home. Turning to a scripture in my Bible, that I had marked on a previous occasion when our other child was so very ill, I read the 23rd Psalm. I found comfort in these words, and lay down to sleep for two hours. I awoke from a very vivid dream. I knew that our child would recover.

I returned to the hospital. Later that evening, when we went in to visit him for the few minutes they allowed, he was alert and looking around. When he saw his dad, he said "Da-Da." We wept simultaneously. Our prayers and those of all our prayer partners had been answered. Perhaps everyone we knew had lifted a prayer for our little angel to survive. I know the Lord saved him for a purpose to serve Him.

I know the Lord kept him to be a help to someone along the way. I gave my child to the Lord that very day and said "Lord" if he is needed in a foreign country, I can let him go, for Your sake. I meant every word that I said that day.

My husband's health began to decline. He was still losing weight, and was now at an all time low of 140 pounds. That was entirely too thin for a 6' man. Since the baby's illness, and the enormous bills that we had amassed, we felt definitely led of the Lord to leave school and return to our old hometown and to the Print Shop. We could resume our work as Tent Makers and work with the deaf there. This was a hard decision to make, therefore we were much in prayer before we made the move.

June of 1964, following the school year, we returned to Mississippi. Ironically, Highway 45 never looked so good. We were going "home."

We resided in a local trailer park in the mobile home that our friends had loaned us for four years. With a family of five, it was entirely too small, and we were forced to seek housing large enough to accommodate all of our growing family.

We sold the trailer and moved into a rental house. We began to pay the friends, a little money each month, for the trailer. They were in agreement with us and fully understood our situation. Dr. and Mrs. John Clark were true blue friends.

Upon returning to the state, we drove through Nettleton to visit Aunt Gert. She still resided at the old home place. I made a decision that day to try and fulfill some of Dad's dreams for me.

I landed a job as an interpreter at Red Raspberry, V.R. in Tupelo.

That fall, I entered Wood Junior College, in nearby Mathiston. I had yet to receive my High School Diploma. However they never questioned me about it. The decision had been made for me to enroll in school and major in elementary education and become a teacher.

I worked three days in Tupelo, and went to school two days a week. Rosie kept the children for us. My husband was working a great deal and we were faring relatively well financially.

Suddenly, I became ill. I awoke one morning to discover that I could not get out of bed. I was terrified. My husband called the doctor, and was told to get me to the hospital immediately. In the emergency room the first question that the doctor asked was whether I had been under stress. My response was that I definitely had been working too hard. I was twenty-five at the time. The doctor ran a battery of tests to determine the exact cause of my inability to move. Three days later I was dismissed to return home with a diagnosis of multiple sclerosis.

I had never heard of M.S., much less knew what to do about it. Rosie came daily to assist with the children. She would help me out of the bed into the tub where I was left to try and work my legs. My arms were ok, but I had difficulty seeing, and my equilibrium was terrible. I had no use of my lower extremities.

I remained this way for several months, until one day, Rosie announced to me, following my morning bath, that the "Lawd had done told her to leave me in the middle of the flo and I would walk." I screamed to the top of my lungs.

I could not walk, and wondered how could she be so callous to do this to me. I stood there for approximately two hours, then finally took one step and fell on my face.

Rosie then held her hands high and said "Miss Dos done been healed uf dat ole 'ralysis. Praise de Lawd!"

I began to slowly recover from my physical problem. A physician in Columbus stated that he felt that I was over-taxing my body, and should get more rest. That, however, was difficult to do with three small boys, working, a Sunday ministry and maintaining a garden.

It was around this time, that we decided to build a new home. Rent was expensive, and we felt that we could acquire a F.H.A. loan.

Much to our chagrin, we were denied the loan, because we

had requested changes in the blueprint of the house plans. I wanted a kitchen built that would be scaled down to accommodate my short stature.

A local businessman hearing of our plight offered to help by assuming the loan, and building the house himself. He owned approximately three acres of land on the outskirts of town. It was located in a new subdivision that was being erected west of town. Anxious to sell the existing property this was one means of doing so.

The entire family piled into our newly acquired automobile and drove out to the wooded area that the kind man owned. It would be an ideal place to raise our three boys. It was located in the country. We could have a garden and the boys could have animals.

Plans began for our dream home. We had a mutual agreement that upon completion of the house that it would be dedicated to the Lord. We had open house, invited all of the church members and our close friends and relatives. A newspaper article in the local newspaper stated that we had been instrumental in having the house built to accommodate me, and we had dedicated it to the Lord, thanks to the Bryan Meat Co. owner of West Point, Mississippi.

1966 began as a good year for us. We were located in a new house, the children loved school, and all of us were on the road to recovery from our health problems.

During the summer months, we would venture to the state of New York where we assisted in a summer camp. The campsite was located near Lake Arrowhead. We averaged one hundred deaf campers for two weeks while we were there. We enjoyed traveling and taking our family on these outings. The boys learned to ride horses, and made numerous friends while at camp.

It was a Christian camp, therefore the boys learned a great deal about the Bible at that time. Those were good times. I could visualize Mommie being very proud of me, as I considered myself a missionary to the deaf. I served as the interpreter, and my husband taught sign language, and other classes. It was a learning experience for the entire family.

Later that year, we were contacted by the Vocational Rehabilitation Department, to consider becoming foster parents to a deaf student at M.S.D. That was when Earl Sandidge, a deaf teenager, entered our lives. At age 17, he had been orphaned, and had other hearing siblings elsewhere.

It was necessary for us to pass state rules and regulations to become bona-fide foster parents. We passed with flying colors, and thereafter were qualified to have other foster children within our home. The deaf foster son spent much of his time at the state school for the deaf. However when he was at home, he seemed to be seeking something more than we had to offer. He wanted to be reunited with his siblings.

We made efforts to locate his sister and brother. His younger brother was residing in a foster home in north Mississippi, but was anxious to move. It seemed ideal, to have the two boys reunited. We were instrumental in making this happen, and when they saw each other, they were like two little puppies. They had been separated so long, and had grown up without seeing each other mature. It was a thrilling sight to see them meet for the first time in over ten years.

Our house was large enough to accommodate all of our now increasing family. I taught the children to be responsible, and assist in keeping the house and yard clean. As a result, I was named "Homemaker of the Year," for Clay County the following year. That was the first real accomplishment where I felt I had been totally responsible for the results.

I began to work once again as an interpreter. Often I would assist at the Print Shop, if they were in need of part-time help. I also started back to school. It was at this time, that a good friend of mine, Bill Woodrick, who was a professor at the University of Tennessee informed me of the "Orientation to Deafness" program at the college in Knoxville.

After much prayer and thoughtful consideration, regarding leaving my family for three months, I took the steps necessary to further my education. Dad would be extremely proud of me now, I knew.

We drove to Knoxville, where I rented a room from the Pastor of a local Baptist church and his wife. They were just like family to me.

A mutual friend of ours who was affiliated with the Home Mission Board of Atlanta, had recommended them to us. I could rest assured that I was in good hands with them while I was there.

Daily the pastor's wife and I would drive to U.T. where we were both in the same class with my friend the professor. That was a real learning experience for me. Now I was having words placed on my pictures. Pictures of the life with the deaf that I had known for over twenty-seven years were now coming to light.

Upon completing my course there, and returning to my home to join my family, I began to accept interpreting engagements. The pay was excellent, therefore, we were able to afford many luxuries of life that had eluded us before. There was only one problem. The assignments separated me from my family. This I did not relish.

We continued our work at the Baptist church, and assisted the deaf in the area as much as possible. We were self-appointed missionaries, often paying our own way, and giving both counseling and financial assistance whenever it was needed.

In the meantime, the superintendent at the Mississippi School for the Deaf informed us that they were experiencing difficulty in securing house-parents to serve in the dormitories following the retirement of some of the staff. He offered us a part-time position there on weekends.

In the fall of 1968, we began to serve as house-parents there. We would travel from our home, to Jackson on Fridays, then return home on Sunday nights to our regular jobs during the week.

This was a hectic time for us, as I was still working on a degree. It had finally been discovered by Wood Junior College, that I had been to college with my deaf husband and served as an interpreter, to the University of Tennessee, and attended their school for one year, part-time, and had not met the entry requirements by having a high school equivalency examination. They, too, realized that I had not been administered the S.A.T. examination.

I journeyed to Itawamba Junior College, located in Fulton, Mississippi to vie for my High School Diploma. Later that month, I was notified, that I was now a full-fledged owner of an equivalency to a High School Diploma. Another of my dreams for Dad had been fulfilled. I had not walked across a stage to receive my diploma, but in my mind, I could see Dad encouraging me to keep on. My dreams would eventually materialize.

I was doing fairly well in my classes, even though I did not have adequate time to study. The children took up much of my time, and I was usually tired by the time they went to bed, and too tired to devote very much time to making good grades. But I was getting by. The commuting itself was very tiresome to me. The trip to Tupelo was thirty-five miles one way, three times a week, and the drive to Mathiston was approximately forty miles one way, twice a week. So I spent a great deal of my time on the road and in the car.

In the spring of the following year, the superintendent of the school offered us a full-time position. Bubba was now living on the campus as he was in charge of the Vocational Rehabilitation Services there. He had received his masters degree from Mississippi State University earlier that year. Mother would be residing next door. Our family would be close to each other once again. I was delighted.

We placed an ad in the local newspaper, expecting our house to be on the market for a lengthy time as with the previous one. However, our prayers were answered. Immediately we received four responses, and had the house sold within a week.

Our fancy Duncan Phyfe furniture was sold, and we kept only the necessary items to furnish an apartment at M.S.D. Loading up the U-Haul, one time I had the feeling that Mommie and Dad were watching from above. This was the close of another chapter in our lives.

The boys had mixed emotions about moving from a mid-size town to such a large city as Jackson. They did not know what would await them there. However in the past, they had never experienced any difficulties in locating and establishing new friendships, therefore I felt they would not have any problems there either. During our part-time work at the school, the boys had already begun to like the idea. They were fascinated by having a gymnasium in their backyard, and a football field in their front yard. We were on our way once again for another chapter in our lives.

10.
THE SECOND FIVE YEARS (MORE BABIES)

The Mississippi School for the Deaf holds many fond memories for "Dummy's Little Girl." I recall having attended football and basketball games, in addition to attending Homecomings there.

As I had stated before, the deaf are very close, and they convene whenever there is an announced gathering of their peers. We were in the heart of all the activities now.

Our apartment was located in the same dormitory that some of my family members had been housed in when they were students there. Our deaf adopted son was a student and the children had good schools to attend nearby.

M.S.D. is located Northeast of Jackson in a rather exclusive part of the city. Many of the children in the neighborhood who attended the same schools with our boys, came from prestigious families. Therefore we knew that they would have nice children with whom to play.

The school year started with a boom. We were located in the Older Boys Dorm, and I was slated to be their house-mother. Having had only boys, I felt that I was rather experienced at dealing with some of their problems.

While we were in college, following the last baby's birth, I had gained a considerable amount of weight. Now I weighed more than I had ever weighed before, however, being at the school, gave me an incentive to make efforts to start a weight reduction plan. Beginning to feel better about myself, and possessing a real feeling of accomplishment, I jumped into my job with both feet. I *KNEW* Dad would be real proud that I was involved in something I liked and loved.

The superintendent at the school had been in charge since 1942. He was a dyed-in-the-wool Miss. State football fan, but at the same time supporting the school for the deaf in all of its endeavors. Some of the teachers who were at the school when my husband was in attendance, were still in the classroom teaching.

Because of our training and sign language expertise we were also given the opportunity to substitute teach whenever there was an emergency or a long-term vacancy which could not be filled until the following year. I was in "Hog Heaven." The children were doing well in school and they loved the campus. They were now having the opportunity of being around their Mama Flo more since she resided next door. They could run over there just any time that they so desired, and she always welcomed them with open arms.

Alumni activities were frequent around the campus. We were all involved with the former students as well as the students on campus. Daily visitors were not a rarity, however we enjoyed them all. The children also had their own private room. They learned to play ping-pong and other games. All five of our boys became very competitive in all of their activities, both at their own school and at the school for the deaf. The deaf boys were like their own siblings and peers. They were enjoying life.

Our hearing foster son, Jack, was an excellent athlete. He was doing exceptionally well at the Junior High School. Ironically, Coach Jack Carlisle, our former neighbor in Nettleton and Bubba's former football coach, was now coaching at Murrah High School nearby. We had high hopes for one of our boys for the following year.

We knew that Coach Carlisle was a disciplinarian on the football field, and with his leadership, our son had the potential to win a scholarship. Our acquired boy was exceptionally good in track—and field events. The entire family was very pleased with him.

The other children were involved in little league sports.

I was again preparing to return to college. Milsaps and Belhaven, both church sponsored colleges, were located in Jackson. I chose to attend Belhaven, because Jean Carlisle was an assistant in the admissions office. I felt more comfortable there, and it was located nearer to the campus where I resided.

Mississippi's renowned poet, Eudora Welty, resided across the street from the college. I was fascinated by her writings, and read many of her books. Many hours were spent in the college library during my off hours at the school for the deaf.

While the children were in school, the majority of my time was devoted to self improvement. I was once again fulfilling a dream.

My family, as usual, was very supportive of me in my efforts to obtain my degree. Often at times, I felt like I was making a career at attending college. I had walked the halls of several, already, and still did not have a "sheepskin in sight."

However, I was not ready to give up, because of the dream that was mine. One that was embedded so deep within my soul that I could not erase it, regardless of how hard I tried.

Dad was still one of my driving forces.

While researching through some poetry books one day, I stumbled across the following poem, written by Amanda Bradley.

Always Have a Dream

> Forget about the days when it's been cloudy,
> But don't forget your hours in the Sun.
> Forget about the times you've been defeated,
> But don't forget the victories you've won.
> Forget about mistakes that you can't change now,
> But don't forget the lessons you've learned.
> Forget about misfortunes you've encountered,
> But don't forget the times your luck has turned.
> Forget about the days when you've been lonely,
> But don't forget the friendly smiles you've seen.
> Forget about the plans that didn't seem to work out right,
> But don't forget to "Always have a Dream."

The poem seemed so appropriate at the time. I was really back on course, and would have my degree in no time at all, I was certain. Elementary Education was my ultimate goal, with Deaf Education as a secondary alternative.

Several workshops for the deaf were being held in neighboring states, and I was invited to interpret. I gleaned much from these meetings, because I was learning more and more about the deaf and their culture. Too, it was opening up new avenues for me to be of service to the ones that I had always adored.

The local club for the deaf had a basketball team that was doing well. They had already won several local tournaments, had proceeded on to the Regional Tourney, won it, then was to vie for the National Tournament in California.

My deaf husband was fortunate enough to accompany the group on the trip. He had a most enjoyable time with the group, as it was his first trip west and especially to the California area. It was also his first cross country flight. I was so pleased that he was going because I knew it would be both an informative and exciting time for him. I had never deprived him of any pleasure with his deaf peers.

Meanwhile back at the dorm, I was left to keep things in order. With the assistance of the live-in assistant house-parent, I experienced no problems. The boys were all obedient and did not attempt to create any disturbances. They were aware that I was in charge, while the head of the household was away.

We purchased a new Plymouth Fury III, a new truck, and a new travel trailer that would sleep six. Our summers were spent either on the farm in New Albany, or at a summer camp in the trailer.

The boys had a tent to sleep in, so it was nice as long as it was not raining, that was when they all piled into the trailer.

Weekends when we were scheduled to have several off-days, we would take our trailer to the Ross Barnett Reservoir near Jackson, and camp a day or two for R. and R. The boys loved to swim and enjoyed fishing while there. They all took to the water like ducks Everyone in the family could swim except me. I was still petrified of water. At times, I would have flashbacks of the incident at Sardis Reservoir. At times it was difficult for me to remain at the campsite alone. However, I knew that I should and could not influence my children in any way regarding my fear of the water.

One day into our second year at the school, we were called to the office and informed that some adjustments had been made in our salary, thereby giving us a financial windfall.

We notified our friends, the Clarks, and mailed them the remainder of the money that we had owed them on the trailer. The one that had been our home for four years while in college.

They later informed us that it was a definite answer to a prayer for them. They were in full-time Christian work and were in need of the money.

Meanwhile, the school was being asked to make drastic changes. We knew the changes were imminent because change was to come to all schools in the south in the early part of the year of 1969.

Integration was not going to be an easy task for anyone. However someone would be destined to lead the way.

We were asked if we would consider moving to the all-black campus across town. The choice of accepting the change or possibly not having a place of employment stared us in the face. We knew it was required by law for integration to transpire one way or another, and the school for the deaf would not be exempt. Naturally we were despondent regarding the possibility of a move from our haven, but we also knew someone had to do it and it might as well be us.

During graduation at the school that year, I collapsed. I was again very ill. I had been working too hard lately, I knew also that I was beginning to feel pressures that I had not experienced before. My back began to hurt and I worried that I might again be having problems with the scoliosis.

I made an appointment with the gynecologist at the nearby medical center. They did a series of examinations, and to my amazement was informed that I was pregnant. AGAIN!

Another dream deferred. College would have to wait. I had destined myself into thinking that the only degree that I would ever receive would be from the "University of Hard Knocks." Perhaps a Ph.D. in the area of Domestication.

Immediately, I began to gain weight. That summer, we attended the state convention on the coast. The following week, the Mississippi Gulf Coast was totally destroyed by Hurricane Camille. If I had a girl, a name had already been chosen, Camille!

That summer, we also attended the camp activities for the deaf at the local ranch. My good deaf friend who had attended college with us gave me one of her little female poodles.

Fearing that I would not deliver a little girl, at least I would have another girl in the house, even if it was a dog. We named the tiny black pup, Dobi, a combination for Do for Doris and Bi for two. She was the love of my life.

We returned from our trip to Tennessee and also New York. I was scheduled for a doctor's appointment, the following week. To my sheer surprise, the physician stated that she could hear two heart-beats. There was a possibility that I was carrying TWINS!

"TWINS!" everyone exclaimed. This was truly possible because of the genetic background that existed within my family. There were several sets of twins on Mother's side of the family. Mother had even predicted that I would have twin boys.

The due date was in the winter. What a Christmas gift that would be!

I completed the school year at Belhaven, and began to make plans for the baby or babies. By now I was thirty, and THIS TIME we both agreed at the doctor's insistence, that this should be my last pregnancy. I certainly did not object.

Continuing to gain weight, I felt that I could not carry the babies until Christmas. However around the middle of October, I became ill with a viral infection in my ears. I suffered day and night. Finally one night, after spending several painful and sleepless nights, we drove to the emergency room at the nearby hospital. The attending physician said that I had an abscess on my eardrum and it would require a minor surgical procedure. I was limited to the types of antibiotics that I could take, because of a tendency toward being highly allergic to medications.

The doctor lanced the eardrum, and I was sent home to recuperate. It was no easy task. Being in pain, caring for a large family of boys, both in the dormitory and my own family, in addition to the pregnancy. There were 45 boys in the dormitory at that time, so we had quite a handful.

Time passed slowly. My sixth month appointment was due. The doctor requested the opinion of another staff physician. While both listened to the heartbeats, I prayed. It was eventually determined that I was carrying only one fetus, and they were hearing my heartbeat and that of the baby's simultaneously. What a relief!

The holidays came, and the family loaded into the automobile with the trailer in tow, sans pregnant mother and baby brother. They headed toward the farm in north Mississippi to hunt wild game.

As our young son remained behind with me to await the new arrival, I felt comfortable knowing that Mother was nearby, and would be of assistance if necessary.

Everything was in order. The baby bed awaited the new arrival. The suitcase had been packed for two months, and all of the tiny clothing was placed in a drawer near our bed. I waited anxiously.

The children would telephone daily for their deaf father to check on me and see how I was progressing. I had requested that my husband attend the birth as this would be the last one. However I felt deep in my heart that he was frightened about the possibility. Therefore, I knew, I would have this baby alone, as I had delivered all of the others. I knew, too, that I faced surgery following this birth. However I waited with eagerness.

New Year's Day, the entire clan of boys arrived on campus. Our family, following an enjoyable two weeks on the farm, hunting game, were refreshed and ready for a new year.

The deaf boys arrived two days later. They were shocked that I was still very much pregnant and did not have a new baby to "show off." "What! No baby girl named Camille?"

I, too, was surprised, because I felt sure that the baby would have been born by now.

A week later, I became very ill with pneumonia. The doctor worried about the safety of the baby, and of my condition. I tried to rest as much as possible, but it was most difficult with chores to attend to in the dormitory.

One of our other children had a birthday. I was almost positive the baby would arrive on that day. My hopes, dreams and prayers were for it to be a little girl. I prayed so hard for a little girl. Foremost, I wanted a healthy baby, but I did so want a little girl to light up my life.

From the time that I was a tiny tyke, I always loved babies. I had my first doll when I was only a few months old. I am told that I carried a doll with me everywhere I went. I loved babies, especially mine.

The day dawned cold and blustery. My avid hunter husband had been hunting daily with his prized dogs. This day, however, he had received a call from the school that one of the teachers would be absent. He chose to substitute for the absentee that day. I did not feel well. However that was not unusual because I had not felt well for some time.

Still fighting the upper respiratory infection. I proceeded to lie down on the couch and eventually fell asleep. Around two p.m. I awoke with a sharp pain. I immediately called the school. The principal informed my husband that he thought the stork was finally on its way. My deaf husband, not realizing the urgency, however, felt it was more important to bring the boys home from their respective schools. So, the Plymouth rushed from school to school gathering up our brood of boys.

He arrived back at the dorm around three. By this time, the boys from the deaf school had arrived. I was in pain, and felt an urgent need to get to the hospital immediately.

Assisting me down the long steps toward the Plymouth, and as we drove away I could see all of the 45 deaf boys and our own sons, standing on the front porch of the dorm, signing the universal sign for "I LOVE YOU." We waved adieu and headed for the Baptist Hospital.

Arriving at the Emergency room at approximately three thirty, a nurse noticing our anxious faces and flying fingers, located a wheelchair and immediately transported me to the Maternity floor. My husband then went downstairs to admissions to complete the necessary papers to admit me and the new addition to the hospital.

The Maternity floor was finally in sight for me. Informing them that I felt certain that I was in the advanced stages of labor, my membranes ruptured. Quickly they placed me on the gurney and wheeled me into the delivery room. The baby was finally coming. WOWEE!!!!

Meanwhile, my husband having completed the preliminaries of having me admitted, came to the Maternity floor in search of his "short wife." He, using sign language, indicated a short woman.

At that time they informed him it was a girl. He said, "No! You do not understand, I am looking for my wife who is here in the labor room." One nurse, sensing that he did not fully understand, wrote it on paper—"It's a girl! You and your wife have a little girl."

He began to kiss all of the nurses, and the female gynecologist as she exited the delivery room. They said they had never seen anyone so excited. They brought her from the delivery room to show her to her father. Her little cries fell on deaf ears. However her blue eyes were unmistakably like mine. "Dummy's Little Girl," at long last had that one long, long dream fulfilled.

A visitor, standing nearby, held a Polaroid camera. Her daddy requested that he take a picture of the baby so he could take it back to the school and show it to the boys, my mother and the students.

Leaving the hospital he drove rapidly to the school for the deaf. The entire student body was in the dining room at 5:00 p.m. for the evening meal. That was when the picture and the announcement was made that our family finally had the long awaited for, beautiful little blue-eyed, curly haired, tiny baby girl.

A baby that would be the apple of her mother's eye and would steal her daddy's heart away. And possibly in the future, fulfill many of the dreams that my dad once had for me. She too would face many of the adversities of "Dummy's Little Girl" because her daddy, like mine was deaf. However, she would have the advantage of numerous innovative ideas now being implemented for the "Deaf World." My girl!

The new addition was then shown to her groggy mother around eight o'clock that evening. I requested that they remove her diaper and covering so I could see all of her little body. Each finger, toe, hand, leg, and her entire body was inspected by this doting mother. The little body of my new baby girl was perfect. With tears in my eyes, I stroked her little head. The nurses did not want me to be near her, because I still had the upper respiratory infection.

Lannie Love, a personal friend of ours, a manufacturing jeweler, was one of our visitors that evening. He brought her a little gold ring with a diamond in the center. The hospital staff placed a sign on her bassinet in the nursery. It read "The only little girl with 50 brothers."

Naturally, everyone wanted to see what the mother looked like after so many children. I felt like the little old lady who lived in a shoe.

My husband loaded the school bus with all of the boys from the dorm the day following the birth. They were scheduled for a field trip that day so naturally they wanted to see the new addition to the family. As they filed into my room one by one, and past the viewing area of the nursery located in the maternity ward, it was a sight to behold. We were all so excited about this new arrival, and it was a joy to share this occasion with the deaf boys.

The little girl now bore the name of my best friend in Nettleton, my husband's sister, my good deaf friend in college, and our dear friend who had allowed us to use their trailer for four years. They were now missionaries to the deaf in a northern state and had no girls, only boys. I was so proud of my child's new name.

My new one was a living doll. She was so tiny and petite. With her blonde hair and blue eyes, she was an exact replica of me. I could not believe that I had finally produced the little girl that I had always prayed and requested of the Lord.

A week later, we left the hospital. Dressed in a beautiful little pink dress a gift from her aunt, her namesake, with a ribbon in her hair, the gold ring on her finger, and a frilly little pair of white booties, wrapped in the soft shawl that Mommie had given me for the other babies, she was definitely all girl.

At my request, we drove by the bank to secure a brand new 1970 penny. I planned to put it away with the other things that I would later gather for her wedding day. She was the apple of my eye. She was special, my one and only little girl. I held her close to my breast and prayed for her, as I had for the others.

Upon arrival at the school for the deaf that cold winter morning, our first stop was at the Academic Building. Naturally we had to show off our new offspring.

Our new baby was naturally an instant hit the minute we arrived. Her big blue eyes appeared to be larger than her face. Eyelashes fluttering, she seemed to vie for attention from the very beginning.

We took this tiny little bundle on to the dorm and introduced her to Dobi. At first, the little pup could not understand our baby's cries. Later, noticing that I would respond when the baby cried, she began to bark each time the baby uttered a sound. Dobi was the baby cry signal for my deaf husband in my absence. If the baby cried or made any sounds, the little poodle would run to him and bark, then run toward the crib where she lay. She was a big help to us.

Dobi would then watch attentively while the newborn was cared for. There seemed to be a bond between the baby and the dog. Similarities were already being established between this little girl and "Dummy's Little Girl."

My husband had never been referred to as "deaf and dumb." He had always resented the name "dummy," and would let it be known to anyone who was so callous to use it. As a child, my father explained to me that there were two connotations to the term dummy. He helped alleviate the hate that I had for the name "dummy."

"Dummy" was my dad's love name, but I did not want my spouse to be branded with a name that he felt was degrading. This was the 70's not the 40's.

As the baby grew older, she became attached to her oldest brother. In fact the very first word that she learned to speak was his name. I have never seen a boy so excited about a child's first word as he was when she looked directly at him and very clearly called him by name.

I would feed the baby with her on one knee, and Dobi on the other. We had a rocking chair that was small enough to accommodate all three of us. In fact it was the same rocker that my Mommie had used to rock me. It had been an heirloom handed down from her mother to my dad, then to me.

After feeding my little one, I would rock her and sing to her as I had the others. As I began to sing, there was one song in particular which had an accompanying choir in the background singing "00000." When she was three months old, she began to mimic me by singing "oooooooo" as I sang the song to her. She, like me, loved music immediately. I thoroughly enjoyed singing and teaching her.

11.
COLLEGE AND MORE DREAMS

She loved her daddy. She could detect his heavy footsteps the minute he entered the long hall in the dorm. She would put her index finger on her forehead depicting the sign for "Father." He loved her too. It wasn't long before she became a daddy's girl.

The day arrived for us to transfer to the former all black campus of the school. We had mixed emotions regarding the move.

The baby was now eight months old. I was back in school at Belhaven, and we had a new challenge. I had fulfilled another dream. "I was going to Darkest Africa," but it would be in the confines of the school for the deaf with little black deaf boys.

We had moved the last of our furniture, and went next door to retrieve Dobi. Dobi was a year and a half old by now. She darted down the hall and outside into the yard. She knew something was amiss, because all of the furniture was gone. Not wanting to be left alone and without her family, she ran into the street. The campus patrolman was making his daily rounds. Dobi ran directly in front of his vehicle. She never had a chance.

Screaming, I ran toward my prize puppy. The ears that had taken the place of my husband's deafened ones were now silenced, too. The patrolman apologized. We knew that it was unavoidable, but how would I tell the other family members who by now were all settling in on the other campus across town.

The patrolman offered to bury Dobi for us. He took her down near the Boy Scout hut on the campus we were leaving, and dug a deep grave for her. Later during the week, we went back and placed a block of marble to indicate the burial plot. Dobi left many memories to our family. They were all pleasant ones.

We were assigned the dormitory for the deaf children entering the first grade. It was a new experience for me to have small deaf boys, but using the skills that I had gathered in raising my own, I felt I could handle them.

These little deaf black boys were quite different than the children that I had worked with previously. I was afraid of them, and they alike were afraid of me. It took some time for us to establish a rapport. However with the help of the other Black house-parents in the other dormitories, we made it through the year.

In the move, our children had been compelled to change

schools. They did not like the schools they were assigned to attend. Integration had affected everyone there including our family. This was definitely a time of change.

I learned many things about the black culture that I had not known previously. Too, they learned about the white deaf culture.

Meanwhile, burning the midnight oil, trying to complete as many of my requirements as possible at Belhaven, attending to the children, working in the dorm and accepting some of the opportunities to interpret for various workshops, began to take its toll on me physically.

Due to being physically exhausted, another upper respiratory infection took its toll on me. The doctor ordered me to bed for six weeks. Naturally, having been so active, it was difficult for me to remain in bed. All three boys pitched in to take over the chores. It was at that time, that I realized the domestic things that I had previously taught them, to cook, clean house and take care of the laundry, were now being put to good use. They were good children.

They did an excellent job, and I was extremely proud of them.

I began teaching all of my children responsibilities at an early age. Instructions began when they were being potty trained. It was during that time that all of the boys learned sign language. They were very skilled at communicating with their deaf daddy and grandmother. Their abilities were comparable to the deaf children, and deaf adults complimented them on their finger dexterity. All of the children, however, stated that they did not want to consider a career of working with the deaf as a lifetime occupation. I feel there was some resentment because so much of our time was devoted to the deaf people with whom we worked.

The newborn was different. She refused to use sign language. Relying on one of the boys or me for communication she refused to use sign language with her daddy.

She would point, and just stand until her needs were met. We dubbed her our "Oralist."

A late walker, she was very dependent on her brothers. They doted on her and gave in to her every whim. She loved it, and so did they. Never objecting to babysit, the three boys were always willing to do what was required to assist their parents. We always worked as a team in whatever endeavor we faced.

The school year came to a close for the deaf. We were called to the superintendent's office and immediately was informed that our position would not be available at the black campus in the fall. We were stunned!

What had we done wrong, or failed to do right?

Our family had never been so stranded before. There had always been a place or someone to turn to in time of need. This was one time that we felt so alone, and really began to depend more on the Lord and His guidance.

The owner of the Print Shop in our old home town, had died rather suddenly of a heart attack a few months earlier. My husband felt at that time he had lost one of his very best friends and mentors. Both he and his wife had been like surrogate parents, offering any type of guidance, financial assistance, or support whenever we needed it. We had known them for more than sixteen years. "You and me against the world," was how we felt at this time in our lives. With Mommie, Dad, and now a former boss, the trusted friend all deceased, we felt a real void in our family.

I immediately began to make contacts with some of the people who had befriended us over the years. We sent resumes to various schools for the deaf all over the nation. I applied for a position as an interpreter in several colleges.

We made a trip to the National Technical Institute for the Deaf located on the campus of the Rochester Institute of Technology in Rochester, New York. The children did not like the area. Therefore I did not accept the position.

Traveling through Washington, D.C., we contacted the pastor with whom I had resided while I was at U.T. in Knoxville. At present he was now President Jimmy Carter's pastor, at the First Baptist Church, in D.C. Having left Knoxville, Tennessee a few years earlier, we thought perhaps he might have a need for a minister to the deaf.

12.
GEORGIA ON MY MIND

The children did not like Washington nor were they impressed with nearby Fairfax County, Virginia.

Upon returning to Jackson, we received a telephone call from an administrator at the Georgia School for the Deaf, located in Cave Spring. They had received our resume. We began to make plans to tow the travel trailer toward Georgia and "size up the place."

Since I had taught all of my children to love music, it was not unusual for us to "kill time" by singing while we traveled. I had also taught them a little game to play while we were all confined to the car on long trips.

The trivial but time consuming game was called "bury the cow." With two children on each side of the back seat of the car, they would attempt to locate cows standing in fields along the highway. The object of the game was to count the number of cows in the pastures along the roadside. Spotting a herd of cattle they would excitedly call out the number of cows that each one had spied in the field. However, if by chance we passed a cemetery located on their side, that would be the cue to "bury their cows." Upon the arrival of our next designated rest stop, the children would then exchange sides, so as to be afforded an equal number of possibilities of cows to their credit. The winners of the game would then be afforded the pleasure of choosing our next place to stop and eat. On this particular trip however, between counting and burying cows, we kept singing the song, "Georgia." Somehow, I knew that the Peach state would soon be our home.

Upon arriving in Cave Spring, the children fell in love with the little town immediately. Ironically, it reminded me so much of Nettleton. The Methodist Church even resembled the one in my old hometown.

The little town, however was swarming with people. All of the children commented that they did not know how a place this small could have so many residents.

Later, we discovered that this was the time allocated for their yearly festival, and a majority of the people we saw were only visitors and not residents. Were our children ever more relieved.

We learned also that almost everyone in the town had some connection with the "deaf school" as the old timers called it. Unlike Nettleton the majority of the people in town could communicate in Sign Language.

This would be an ideal place to rear the children. A place where my deaf husband would be comfortable around his peers and hearing people could communicate and understand his deafness. We could attend a church where there was a deaf ministry and perhaps we could assist in that ministry.

This was another change, another dream, and another chapter in the life of "Dummy's Little Girl."

Our first chore was to locate housing for our family of six. We had parked the travel trailer at a campground on Weiss Lake in nearby Alabama. The children loved the water and they would have chosen to live there permanently. It was however, very crowded in the 17' travel trailer, when we gathered for a meal.

We began to ride around the countryside on a daily basis searching for the "perfect" house.

An employee at the school, a wonderful Christian lady, learned of our search and informed one of the staff at the school to notify us that she had two houses that were on the market to be sold. My husband and my dad's namesake were in town at the time, and went out to look at both of them and talk with another soon to be surrogate mother, Mama Tressie.

They returned to the campsite very excited. They wanted all of us to accompany them to the perfect little nook for our family. It was located directly on the back-waters of Lake Weiss, on Big Cedar Creek and was nestled on a dead end road in the country.

We journeyed to their "find." Yes! it was an ideal place, but it was very small. It was a cabin consisting of two small bedrooms, a large uncompleted addition on the end of the house, and a den and kitchen combination. It had one small half-size bath, with no tub, only a shower stall.

The children and their dad loved it. However, I did not, but was reluctant to say so. I had always been so afraid of water that I had never attempted to take a shower. The water coming from above, splashing on my head and face, would make me panic.

I had never been one to stand in the way of my family's happiness, and I certainly was not going to start now.

13.
SLEEPY HOLLOW ROAD, GEORGIA

The thoughts of having such a large body of water near my children all the time, concerned me. I could visualize the toddler slipping away and falling into the creek and drowning before anyone could retrieve her. Not a single child of ours had ever shared the same fear of water that I had experienced over the years. I experienced mixed emotions about their love of the water from time to time.

Regardless, of my negative feelings, we purchased the cabin on the the dirt road appropriately named Sleepy Hollow. Everyone with the exception of me was pleased and happy with the decision.

It was truly an ideal location and had numerous possibilities of being remodeled into a lovely and comfortable abode for our family. We were, however, aware that money would be the main deterrent in renovation procedures in the near future. By accepting the position at G.S.D., we had accepted a drastic cut in salary. We all knew that we were in for some difficult times ahead, financially.

Often, I would look out of the single, small kitchen window, overlooking the creek, and cry. Somehow, I just could not overcome my fear of the water. My dad's tragic drowning, was still imprinted deep within the passageways of my memory. However, I prayed that someday I would overcome my phobia, and muster up enough courage to learn to swim. That was another one of my secret desires and dreams. Dad would be so proud of me if I could accomplish that feat.

The children found numerous ways to entertain themselves in Sleepy Hollow. They were fascinated by the creek and what its waters held. Immediately, they also wanted a dog to watch the cabin. It wasn't long before they found an old mutt that everyone loved and adored. The Heinz 57 variety did not have papers, nor did it resemble the show dogs that my spouse had brought from New York, but he was a good watchdog, and barked at the right times. That was the important thing. He was justly named Big Mac, because he thought he was a human and a bona-fide member of the family.

Doris Isbell Crowe

Mommie with the grandchildren: back row, left to right, Joe Rieves, Dorothy Isbell, Kathryn Isbell, Sally King, and Ruby King; front row, Betty Jean Rieves, Hal Rieves, Doris, Mommie, Cora Haney (in Mommie's lap), "Bubba," and Joe King.

Sitting in front of Dummy's Jeep in 1948 are (left to right) Aunt Velma's children, Cora, Rebecca, and Nell Haney, with Doris Mae and Carl "Bubba" Isbell.

Doris Mae in first grade in Nettleton, Mississippi.

Dad, "Bubba," Aunt Katie's grandson, Mother, and Doris at age eleven.

Dorothy Hester, Doris at age fourteen (in her first store bought dress, a gift from Aunt Toy), Judy Cook, and Helen Ramage.

Trip to Florida, 1952. Mr. and Mrs. J.O. Cook (Aunt Toy and Uncle J.O.), Judy Cook Pryor, and Doris.

Mrs. Gertrude McDuffie Roberts (Aunt Gert) with Doris' daughter.

Florence Isbell and Mattie Nelson Massengill (Granny), 1950.

Doris at age fourteen with cousins Bert Jones of Huntsville, Alabama, and Julius "Tack" Moore of Meridian, Mississippi, 1953.

Carl Moorehead Isbell, Sr.—"Dummy"—in his shoe shop in Nettleton, Mississippi, 1950.

Doris receives her degree from Floyd College, Rome, Georgia, in June 1973.

Friends Glenda and Alvin Couey and Nancy Langston Barker.

Grammy and Paw-Paw Crowe with five-year-old granddaughter Jennifer Crowe.

Dolla Crowe Cape, Allen's eighty-five-year-old mother, "Nana."

Elaine King, Mama Flo, Aunt Katie King, and Elaine's husband, Joe King.

Doris and son John McDonald at the cowboy wedding.

Allen and Doris Crowe, "The Hi-Lows."

Doris (center) with neighbors Navaughnia and Sam Kerr.

The Wedding Party. To the left of Doris Crowe (the bride), and Allen Crowe (groom), are (left to right) the children in front: Jennifer Hillman, Celisse McDonald, and Jordan Williams; behind them (left to right) are Beverly Williams, Teena Cagle, Don McDonald, Alice McDonald, and their infant, Chelsey McDonald. To the right of the bride and groom are (left to right) Dolla Crowe Cape, Pete Ryther, Jerry Cape Oakes, Nathan Oakes, Faye Cape-Ryther, and Rev. Dewey Bailey.

Connor and Myrtle Dillard celebrate their twenty-fifth wedding anniversary.

One of our first visitors to our cabin were the Dillards. A childless deaf couple who resided in town. We had numerous things in common. Mr. Dillard reminded me so much of my dad it was unbelievable. He was the shoe repairman and teacher of special students at the school. A comical man, we all learned to enjoy his antics when he and his lovely wife made visits to our home.

Another couple who came to visit were the Fanshaws. He was the Baptist State Missionary to the deaf. His wife was a teacher at the school, and they had two children, a boy and a girl, near the same ages as our two oldest boys. We liked them immediately and eventually established a strong relationship with them.

The Cave Spring School and G.S.D. were scheduled to open simultaneously. We, however, managed to get all of our boys registered on time at their respective schools.

G.S.D. was a historic old school. I was assigned to be a houseparent with older girls, and my husband was to work with the younger boys. We were scheduled to work opposite shifts. He would work three and a half days, and I was to work the other three and half days. This gave us the opportunity to have at least one parent at home with the children while the other worked. We seldom saw each other. Our days off were few and far between.

We were looking forward to making new friends; getting involved in the activities of the deaf; becoming active in church work; and being supporters of our boys in their activities at their school. Our expectations materialized and we were not disappointed whatsoever.

Money was scarce. We did not seem to have enough to go around. With two teenagers in high school; a deaf foster son away in college at Gallaudet in Washington, D.C.; one child in elementary school; and one toddler in the nursery; we struggled to make ends meet. We were compelled to sell the family's prized truck to aid us financially.

The first winter, the children and I all became ill with a viral infection. It was one that we could not shake, by any means. I tried every remedy that was suggested to me, but none of them seemed to work. I even tried the banana remedy that Mommie had used on me at one time. We had finally decided that the sickness was attributed to contamination in the well water. We had the local sanitation inspector from the Health Department to perform a perk test. To our dismay, it was discovered that our well was definitely contaminated, and we had all contracted some sort of bacterial infection that had settled in our intestines.

The children's dad was the only one of the family who did not become ill, therefore it fell to his responsibility to care for all of us. One evening, while I was conversing on the telephone with Wanda Fanshaw, I noticed that the toddler, began to experience difficulty in breathing. Shortly, she began to convulse and become limp. I was horrified. My husband was at work, and I had no transportation as we now possessed only one vehicle. Wanda heard my screams on the other end of the telephone line, and informed her husband to come to my aid to transport the baby to the hospital.

Meanwhile, Wanda notified the school of my dilemma, and my spouse immediately left the school to meet us at the hospital. The baby had suffered an acute reaction to the medication that I had been administering to her for the viral infection. I thought surely we had lost her, but the Lord protected her little life by providing the right people at the right time.

The virus had weakened us all and caused us to lose a considerable amount of weight. For several months we all looked very sickly and in poor health.

Spring came, and we were finally over the physical problems that had plagued us a few months earlier. Springtime on Sleepy Hollow Road was a sight to behold. Flowers seemed to burst from nowhere and the once drab bushes became colorful and bright. The road was finally paved to make travel much easier for all of the residents in our little cove.

14.
THE THIRD FIVE YEARS

We had all completed one school year in Georgia. Summer was upon us. My husband and the boys mustered up enough odd jobs around town to supplement our income. One day while riding around the countryside, we stumbled across a large blackberry patch. Plans were made for the entire family to pick berries and sell them.

When the residents in town heard that we were selling blackberries, at $5.00 per gallon, we began to receive numerous orders. That first year, we picked and sold one hundred gallons of the black fruit that grew so plentiful on the Georgia hillside.

The proceeds from the sale of the berries went to purchase each child a chair for our lone kitchen table. In addition, we also bought a set of new tires for the only automobile that we owned. We all worked together as a team.

Picking blackberries was an annual event for us each year around July, for four years. We were known as the professional berry pickers. We knew how to seek orders, prepare to go to the "patch," pick the berries with few leaves, and deliver them to the waiting customers before nightfall.

Those were good times for our little family. We enjoyed each other's company. We laughed, cried and prayed a lot during that time.

Fall came, and I joined the children by becoming a student once again. I, hopefully, was on the road toward completing my academic goal this time.

One thing for certain, I would not have another baby, so that was some consolation.

Floyd Junior College located approximately eleven miles away had a Deaf Education program. I enrolled as a part-time student. Working on the night shift at G.S.D., I would leave my job at 8:30 a.m. and travel to "Six Mile," where the college was located.

There I would attend classes from 9:00 a.m. until 1:00 p.m. Following my last class, I would then drive the 13 miles toward Sleepy Hollow. Home. Where I could sleep until the children arrived in the afternoon.

I would awake, prepare their meal, direct them in clearing the table and washing the dishes, then return to bed for a few more hours of rest prior to resuming my duties at G.S.D. at 11:30 p.m.

Those were strenuous times for me, but I knew that it would be worth it in the long run. It seemed that "Dummy's Little Girl" was forever having dreams deferred.

1973 would be a year of numerous changes in all of our family. I had made several good friends during the past two years. They seemed to be the kind of people I could depend on for anything at any time.

Nancy Barker, a counselor and interpreter at G.S.D.; Wanda Fanshaw, a teacher, interpreter and wife of the Missionary to the Deaf; Rev. Dewey Bailey, Methodist Minister, Ombudsman and Methodist Missionary to the Deaf at G.S.D.; and, as I mentioned previously, the Dillards.

Nancy was the kind of person who could do just about anything. She was skilled at any task that she attempted, and had more talent in her little finger than I had in my whole body. She really encouraged me to go on to school regardless of the obstacles.

Nancy and her husband Gene had no children of their own, but I do believe the entire area of children had chosen them as surrogate parents. Nancy and I were the same age, shared so many of the same interests, and could laugh and cry together. Most important of all, she was a fine Christian woman and I could rely on her for a listening ear at anytime day or night.

I bent her ear so much that I often became ashamed to make a call, but I knew she would "hear me out," and always take the time to give me some encouragement. She was much taller than I, and the picture of loveliness in everything that she attempted. Nancy was unique and that is why I liked her so much.

We have remained constant friends over the years, and she had been a mainstay during my numerous trials and tribulations. She was just like the childhood friend that I had in Nettleton. Judy and she shared many of the personality traits that I admired in both of them. Most of all Nancy, like Judy, was interested in me. She would give me that extra push, when I was down and out.

Wanda, too, was a good friend. She became ill the second year after we moved to Georgia. Having to be hospitalized, it was discovered that she had a malignancy that had spread rapidly, and she was now terminally ill. My heart was broken. I loved Wanda.

I would visit Wanda each day on my way to school. We would pray with each other, and never failing, she encouraged me to keep on with my school work. She, like me, had in the past experienced a phobia to water. She encouraged me to take swimming lessons so I could overcome it as she had.

Later that year, Wanda succumbed to the ravages of the disease that she fought so hard to overcome. Her funeral was held in the First Baptist Church of Cedartown, however I had the flu and could not attend.

I wrote a poem in her memory, as I had for the others so close to me. It was read in closing at her final service.

Wanda was laid to rest on the hillside at the Cave Spring Cemetery. Wanda was special.

DEDICATED HANDS
by
Doris Isbell Crowe

A deaf child stood in silence
As the class was led in prayer,
She watched the hands of Teacher
Conveying the words with care.

As folded hands said, "Amen"
To end the talk with God,
The child then signaled Teacher
Which was acknowledged with a nod.

I have an important question
To ask about our prayer,
"Does Jesus know sign language?
Does He hear my prayer up there?"

Teacher's fingers answered quickly,
"You should never have that fear,
The folks who live in Heaven
All talk, sing songs and hear."

The child then smiled so sweetly,
Turning slowly to her chair,
To this experienced teacher

Such questions were not rare.

Her hands dedicated to the deaf so fully
Oft answering questions without rest
Just as Jesus's hands were nail scarred
For those He loved the best.

Now Teacher's hands no longer
Give forth messages of God's love.
Those hands now rest contentedly
In His hands, in Heaven above.

Rev. Bailey depended on me for various and sundry things. He was a preacher's preacher. He and his lovely wife Hattie could be called on for prayer or any other type of assistance in time of need.

Later, when one of our children was in the first grade, her teacher inquired as to what was her mother's profession. She replied that her mother worked with beans. (She had overheard me saying that I felt that all of my adult life had been spent working with human beings.)

She had misinterpreted the word beings as being beans. She also informed her teacher that her mother's faith was Baptist every day except Friday, and on that day she was a "Preacher Bailey Methodist." Of course that brought a chuckle from all of those who knew our family.

I was in the final month of Junior College. If things went well, I would be walking down the aisle at last in June and receiving my Associate Degree in Deaf Education. I would be the first recipient of that honor at Floyd College, so I was anxiously awaiting the day.

In May of that year, I was nominated by one of my sons, as Mother of the Year, for Rome and Floyd County. One of the local radio stations had promoted the idea, and he had submitted my name.

To my surprise, I was chosen from more than 300 entries. We were all jubilant at the announcement. I was pictured in the paper with him, and the Disc Jockey. Receiving numerous prizes and awards, it was the first time that I had ever felt like a "Queen for a Day." Mommie and Dad would have been proud of me, had they been present. It was the culmination of a year of hard work for me, attending school, working and taking care of the family.

One of our close relatives became very ill in the month of June. Another trip to Mississippi was scheduled. By this time, I was exhausted, as was everyone in the family. It seemed that I might be compelled to postpone the graduation until the fall term. I just could not be this close and not be able to finally get at least one degree.

Finals at Floyd College were exhausting. I survived. On the final day of selections for potential graduates, I was informed that I would be a candidate for graduation.

There was jubilation on Sleepy Hollow Road that day. I called every relative and friend that I had to share the good news. I had finally made it!

On that beautiful June day in 1973, I was the first in line. I stood the tallest. Many of my friends and all of the family had decided to attend the ceremonies to watch me walk across the stage and fulfill one of my lifelong dreams. Mommie and Dad were watching from somewhere, I knew. There had to be joy in Heaven, because I felt certain they would have been delighted. I was, and knew that they must be sharing in that joy.

Following the ceremonies, I was informed by the Administrators that a Federal program for the hearing impaired would be implemented soon, and I would possibly qualify for the position as interpreter, and tutor for the hearing impaired at F.J.C. Another dream fulfilled.

As I lay in my bed that night, I thanked the Lord for His guidance in seeing me through all of the trials of getting my Associate degree. My deaf husband lay beside me, quiet as usual, sound asleep. I could not talk to him in the dark and tell him how very excited I was. That was the way it had always been in the "Deaf World."

There must be a light to communicate. Also if there is a light on, the deaf person usually has difficulty in sleeping, therefore they are acclimated to light whereas hearing people are acclimated to sound.

My parents had lived this existence. I, too, had lived the same way for thirty-three years.

The silence in our house was often deafening when the children were not around.

Floyd College was a very nice place to work. All of the professors had either served as one of my instructors, or I had interpreted for a hearing impaired student in their class at one time, or another.

All of the children were doing fine, with the exception of one of my sons. Another son was in Arkansas, residing with a relative, and working with his brother-in-law. Another child was doing well in school and working part-time. One of the younger ones was in the gifted program at school and excelled in every endeavor that he pursued. The baby was in nursery school and learning also. However, the son who was having problems, at the age of 15 was the same height as was his brother five years younger. He was going to be even shorter than I. At 3'8", he was very tiny for his age.

Being a concerned mother regarding his height, a newspaper article in the Atlanta stated they were conducting a survey in an effort to locate individuals who were of short stature. Emory Hospital in Atlanta had received a Federal grant to offer qualified individuals the opportunity to participate in a Growth and Research Development Clinic. The director of the program was a Dr. Rudman.

I called Nancy and asked her opinion about the possibilities for him. She recommended that I "go for it." She knew how very concerned I was about him and the fact that he was smaller than other boys was affecting his behavior.

My next move was to contact Dr. Rudman at Emory. We were instructed to bring our boy to the hospital for an evaluation to determine if he would qualify for the program. There would be no cost to us, however he would be required to take growth hormone shots as a participant in the program. We were informed also that these are very painful, and the hormones were derived from the pituitary glands of cadavers used in research programs.

Our short son listened in awe as the doctor explained the procedure to me. I interpreted all of the information to my deaf husband so he would be fully aware of what the young teenager would be required to endure.

With sheer determination our dark-haired little boy had no

reservations about entering the program. He would be absent from Cave Spring School, however he could enroll in the outreach program for children located at nearby Eggleston Hospital for children. He was gung-ho on the idea.

The following month, gathering up all of his toys, books, pajamas, cut-off jeans, and other personal belongings, we "moved" him to Emory. He was scheduled to remain there for six weeks at a time.

A very brave son he was. I called him daily to check on his progress. It was at this time that they discovered he had a blood disorder, possibly stemming from birth, identified as leukeopenia. We were all stunned at the discovery, and also to be told that it was possibly terminal. I could not visualize losing him, the only child who resembled my dad the most, his namesake.

The doctor in charge informed us later in the week, that they were planning to attempt a bone-marrow transplant. However, they needed a compatible donor. All of the children accompanied his dad and me to the lab at Emory. It was determined that one other child and I had compatible bone marrow, but his sibling was too young to endure the painful procedure, therefore I was the chosen donor.

The following week, I entered Emory Clinic for a battery of tests. At the end of the week, the bone marrow transplant was performed.

We would not know for several weeks if it would be successful or not. Enduring so much pain we were concerned about him. There was noticeable evidence that he was growing. He began to mature almost overnight, growing facial and body hair. His hands and feet also began to develop. Our little son was finally growing up.

Several months later, it was determined that the bone marrow transplant had been successful. Our prayers were answered and his medical problem was definitely in remission.

May of 1978, now a young man, John Carl McDonald graduated from Cave Spring High School. He stood 5'2" tall. He had grown that much from the months he had spent away from home, and it was worth every minute of it to him.

One of his goals was to join the Air Force. He passed the examination, and was well on his way to becoming an airplane mechanic. He, like my dad, had overcome adversities. However, he would not be stranded with extremely short stature that had once plagued him. This was our boy, one that has always been special.

John remained in the Air Force for two years. With an honorable discharge in hand he returned to the Cave Spring area to work.

In the meantime, one of our older boys had met and married a beautiful young lady. They were residing in a nearby town. My husband of twenty years had suffered three heart attacks within a six month period. We were all very concerned about his health. Following the third attack, he was convinced that it was necessary to have a heart catherization procedure. I accompanied him into the operating room for the cath. Interpreting always came easy for me, however this was one of the most difficult situations that I had ever faced.

I had remained with him while he was confined to the Coronary Care Unit for a week. There was no bed for me to lie on, therefore I slept on the floor or in a chair nearby. The doctors permitted it, because he was deaf, and they felt he would improve more by my presence.

Two weeks later, and in a weakened condition, he was sent home to recuperate. At 45, it was no easy task to keep him occupied, and calm, simultaneously.

I remained on the staff at Floyd College. A long-time friend of mine contacted me about auditioning for a position on the television program, Hee-Haw. They were searching for someone to fill in for the absence of one of their regulars. The director of the program had offered me the opportunity to be in one of the shows. One of my sons accompanied me to Nashville, where we rubbed shoulders with all of the stars from the "Opry." This was one dream of dad's.

It was not to be. I was called back home for an emergency.

My husband's health began to improve. Over the years, he and the boys had performed handyman work for the people in Cave Spring. Often, he would do very strenuous work. This could not be done anymore. Now earning extra money would be up to the children and me.

Floyd College was a place of learning, teaching and activity for me. Now we had one of the new pieces of equipment that would enable the hearing impaired (deaf) to communicate via telephone, with someone who had a compatible machine.

The most enjoyable time of my life was in 1975. This was the very first Mother's Day of our life that I could telephone my own mother and wish her a happy Mother's Day. We both cried.

However this new apparatus opened up new means of communication. Since Mother owned a T.D.D. (as they were referred to), she would often call and inquire as to what was happening on the soap operas. She had now joined the world of the hearing . . . the telephone ringing.

Following the missionary's death, I had purchased her big upright piano. One of my children had inherited a natural ability for the piano, and could play both by ear and music. We took advantage of an excellent music teacher who lived nearby.

My dreams for this child, were those that Dad had for me. Tiny and petite, she could not reach the foot pedals, however this did not deter her stamina in tickling the ivories.

This child, too, could sing. All of my children had inherited the ability to harmonize, and we enjoyed many a songfest around the piano.

Just like my dad, their dad would only sit and watch our faces.

All of the children loved boats, swimming and water skiing. I disliked it immensely, but tolerated it for their sake.

Several motorcycles, go-carts, and a ski-boat were among the other items we began to accumulate around the house.

Our children had been riding the motorcycle with their dad since the age of three. He would bring the baby home from nursery school following his work at G.S.D. Our youngest appeared to be afraid of nothing. The faster they would travel, the louder the laughter. So very tiny, the child appeared to be a little doll riding on the bike with both her brothers and dad.

Later that year, one of the teenagers had a very frightening experience when he and a friend hit a rough place on the highway and wrecked one of the bikes. Fortunately, they escaped with only cuts and bruises. That seemed to be par for the course with a house full of boys. Teenagers seem to want to experiment at everything.

Late one afternoon, the boys' dad noticed that some boys

including ours had gathered at the end of Sleepy Hollow Road. There was something fishy about their demeanor.

Driving down to the end of the road, he observed them checking the trunk of our little Renault. Immediately, the boys all began to pile into the car, making efforts to escape a dad's watchful eye.

However, even though he was deaf, he intervened and requested that they open the trunk. To his surprise, it held a full case of toilet tissue. The boys were planning to "roll yards" that night. Their plans were changed drastically when "pop" confiscated the "loot."

Our rather large family was not required to purchase Scott Tissue for several months following that episode.

The tiny musician in our family continued to play the piano, and enter recitals. We attended each one of them. Their deaf daddy would accompany me and watch them as they performed. This reminded me so much of my mother and dad. The music was beautiful, but it fell on deaf ears. His only option was to watch his little children and their antics.

Christmas came, and because I felt we could afford it, we purchased a new spinet piano. I loved the new piano. The musical whiz and I learned to play duets together, just like my music teacher and I had done many years ago.

The older piano was donated to the Cruselle Freeman Church for the Deaf in Atlanta. It, like "Dummy's Little Girl's" piano would spend its final years serving as a musical instrument in a church.

We were all very active in our church and attended all of the services. Many of the deaf children were attending our church from the Georgia School for the Deaf, and I was teaching a Sunday school class to the deaf. We were doing missionary work again.

That year my husband was ordained as the first "deaf" deacon at one of the local churches. This made us very proud of him and his accomplishments. Later in the summer, he was elected as an officer of the Georgia Baptist Conference for the Deaf. The following year, he was chosen to lead the Christian deaf in the state of Georgia. He was a born leader and a good leader. He implemented numerous innovative ideas regarding interpreting and services to the deaf.

15.
THE SOUVENIR KNIFE

Our children always enjoyed life. Their sense of humor was second to none when we gathered for family outings.

One such incident will forever be ingrained in our memories. It was the famous "souvenir knife."

One of our dear friends and neighbors had been on vacation to the Smokies and had brought the children a souvenir. It was a knife that had every kind of contraption nameable attached to it. We placed it in the dash of the car to use in case of emergencies.

We were planning a trip to Jackson, Mississippi to visit Mother. Their daddy was scheduled to work, therefore he could not accompany us. So the four children and I began our voyage toward the Magnolia State with the protection of our "souvenir knife."

Little did we know how valuable that knife would become before we arrived back home. Its first chore was to repair a loose screw to the window in the car. Secondly, the baby fell asleep, with gum in her mouth. Everyone knows what happens to gum when one has it in his mouth and he falls asleep. Having very long hair at that time, our only choice was to retrieve the knife.

Another child having a sudden call from nature while we were several miles from nowhere on the interstate, had to "go." Trekking back from the woods, he announced that he had broken the zipper to his pants. Welllllll---. Out comes the "knife" to make the needed repairs.

One would think the story would end right here, but no! The "knife" still had life to come.

Lunch time came. We decided to stop and buy a box of chicken for the bunch. Would you know, there were no knives in the box.

Stopping at a roadside park, we took the "knife," cut the bag and box the chicken had been placed in and made a make-shift cover for the table. Some of the chicken pieces had to be cut, so out came "Old Trusty."

It began to rain. The older son had been driving the Plymouth, but I felt more secure with me driving in the wet weather. The windshield wipers began to squeak. In unison the kids all yelled "get the souvenir knife." Once again, it had performed well under pressure.

The "knife" was becoming so popular that it was not being housed in the dash anymore, it had a warmer place of residency. The boys began to take turns keeping it in their pocket.

Nearing Jackson, we noticed a funny sound from the bottom of the car. Fearing that it was the muffler, one of the boys exited the automobile to discover that we had driven over a piece of plastic and it had adhered to the heated muffler.

The call came out "Who has the "knife?" Being retrieved from a little boy's pocket, it served its purpose once again.

Finally, completing our journey, we arrived in Jackson. Their first request of their grandmother was to secure a small cotton-lined box for the "souvenir knife." Puzzled at such a request, she accommodated them.

Arriving home, armed with gifts from Mama Flo, the "souvenir knife" had now been inducted into our family's "Hall of Fame."

The children usually had other children around them most of the time. They were the type of kids that loved to have fun and enjoy life.

We purchased another boat, and made daily visits to Brushy Branch to swim or water ski. All of the children loved the water, and we enjoyed being in their company when they were having so much fun.

Fun times usually followed days of hard work. We all worked together as a family unit. The additions to the house were our main projects.

I had borrowed enough money to build a large storage building, combination workshop for my better-half and the boys. It was 24' by 50', large enough to accommodate all of their vehicles, the boat and my spouse's never ending array of work tools.

One stormy night, about a month after the erection of the "shop," a huge gust of wind swept the entire building into the water behind our house. All that was left standing was the boat, very precariously leaning on the edge of the foundation. Everything else was in the waters of Cedar Creek.

With winds gusting up toward 60 miles per hour, the boys

and my husband went out into the dark to survey the damage. Fearful that trees might fall on them, they all donned all available football and motorcycle helmets.

I called the police, for fear that there might be downed power lines as there was no electricity available.

You can imagine the look on the officers' faces when they arrived and saw all these boys and young men, including this deaf man giving orders with his fingers, with helmets on their heads.

One of them replied, tongue in cheek, not realizing that their dad was deaf stated, "anyone who dresses like that and wants to engage in playing sports in a storm like this one, boy! I hope your team wins."

Later the following day, we rounded up several friends and formed a human chain to retrieve all of the lost articles from the creek. If it had not been so sad, seeing all of our belongings soaking wet, it might have been somewhat humorous.

Regardless, we thanked the Lord that we had been spared. The storm could have very easily taken the house instead, and it could have been our bodies they were retrieving rather than tools, mowers, motorcycles, bikes, and the like from the creek.

It took us several months to dry out all of the various and sundry things that were dragged from the murky, snake infested waters of the creek. Following each heavy rain, other items would come afloat. We knew that when fall came, and the rains ceased the water would recede. That would be the time that would enable them to dig into the mud and retrieve the remainder of their lost valuables and their prized "junk" from the creek bed.

That summer, we made another addition to our house. This time a kitchen was scaled down to accommodate my height. I could now reach the kitchen sink without standing precariously on a stool. All of the children could reach the lower cabinets, even the little one was not exempt from washing dishes anymore.

This particular year, we acquired a T.D.D. machine in order for my deaf husband to communicate with the other deaf in the community. The children could call home on the T.D.D. from any compatible machine and "talk" to their dad.

Prior to our purchase of this machine, we had to rely on

"hearing" people to interpret for us, or as a deaf man, he would surmise some means of giving us a code on the telephone.

I recall on one occasion when we had been on a party-line, he called home to inform me that he would be working late. We had developed a code. By using a heavy instrument, we could tap the mouthpiece of the phone, and he could hear the knocks and determine the message. One tap meant "yes," two taps meant "no," three meant "bring bread," four meant "bring milk."

Late one night, a person on our party-line picked up the phone and began to talk. It was obvious that he had been imbibing in some strong spirits. I tried to explain to him what I was doing. My deaf husband on the other end of the line did not know what was transpiring, therefore he began to beat harder on the phone. In desperation, the party-liner said to me, "Hey lady, I don't know what you are trying to do, but I think for sure, I am drunker than I thought I was." When my spouse arrived home, we both had a good laugh about the party-line of the "hearing world."

16.
"G."

The smallest son was the first of the boys to complete the repairs on his motorcycle following the storm. The old dirt bike was his pride and joy. He would ride up and down Sleepy Hollow Road, and "walk" that thing just like a bicycle. He was feisty and loved to be an "Evil Knievel."

One of his very best friends was G. His family treated our boy just like family. In fact, his mother, adored our son as much as she did her own.

G. was 24 and our young man was 19. They spent time together on their dirt bikes riding in the flatwoods. I did not worry when the boys were at "the other mother's" house, for I knew he was in good hands.

August 7, 1977 dawned and it was a beautiful summer day. One that would easily find some people picnicking. Our ever growing boy chose not to attend church that day. He wanted to ride with G. (Garry Gladden).

Making arrangements to meet at the flatwoods near the Georgia Kraft property, they planned to ride the dirt bikes on all of the secluded trails. They had parked their vehicles several miles away in a cove where they would not be disturbed.

G. had failed to get his helmet prior to the first ride. His friend insisting that he go back to the truck and get his helmet, they all decided to follow.

Exiting the flatwoods, they were headed for a long stretch of pavement before the dangerous curve leading to the cove. Our boy on his newly repaired bike was leading the four out of the riding area, and G. passed him. Competitive as they were, he hit the pedal to make his bike go faster than his friend.

Rounding the curve, he saw G.'s bike in the ditch. A carload of children and their parents were on the other side of the road.

He had tried to avoid the sightseeing family as they rounded the curve, and had hit them head on.

Our son, the one who had endured months of pain, jumped off his bike to go to G.'s aid. He held G. in his arms and prayed for him. As the other boys arrived, they felt a need to call an ambulance immediately. However, it was too late. G. had died in the arms of his very best friend.

My father's grandson, was devastated. "How would he tell his second momma?" Her only boy, her pride and joy was now gone. But our brave one felt a need to do that.

He, covered with the blood of his best friend, requested the police to accompany him to the friend's house. His mother was always at home where she spent most of her time caring for a mentally retarded sister. His words were "G.'s gone."

My dad's grandson was an emotional wreck. He had been asked to serve as a pallbearer for the funeral. Feeling that he needed to do that since it would be the last favor he could do for a very good friend, he stood tall like a man.

G. was special to our boy. He loved life, just like our beloved son. His death seemed so untimely, but his mother accepted it as any Christian would. My son's heart ached for the family. He said numerous times that it should have been him instead of his friend.

This reminded "Dummy's Little Girl" of her own heartache.

I had been employed at Floyd College for four years. My job entailed a variety of responsibilities, and I thoroughly enjoyed each task. The Deaf Education program was making progress, and new students were enrolling each quarter.

The director of the program, several deaf students and I were featured on a series of television programs within the state. I was selected to develop a Sign Language Program to be aired each week on the local television station. This was a dream come true.

My health began to fail again, and I began to experience numerous physical problems. The doctor advised me to have another surgical procedure performed. It was not an easy time for me and I missed some days at work. But the Lord was good.

Later, in the year, the school was informed that the Federal grant would not be renewed the following year for the Deaf Education program. I knew it would mean that I would be without employment, but I knew also that it would be in God's hands.

Each time that I had secured employment it appeared that I would have a job better than the previous one. I was relying heavily on the same kind of faith that I had exhibited years before.

We were in the process of renovating the house again, and it seemed that the timing was all wrong for me to be unemployed, but we survived.

A friend informed me of an interpreter's position with the Floyd County School System. I applied, and was readily accepted. The Lord had intervened once again on our behalf.

The year spent interpreting at Pepperrell High School for a deaf student was an enlightening experience. I made new friends and gathered a world of information within the classes. The administrators were friendly to me and the school was a nice place to work, however there were no benefits. I was just a free-lance interpreter.

The Floyd County Court System had utilized my services on numerous occasions. I had been secured to interpret for deaf litigants in various court cases. That was a most interesting challenge, however, it was only part-time. I was seeking full-time employment with benefits. I asked the Lord to provide, and He did.

The following year, I began to have more physical problems

requiring another surgical procedure. It appeared that I was spending more and more time in the hospital. Each time that I had surgery, it would weaken me. I asked the Lord to spare me the pain and suffering that I must endure. He answered my prayer and gently the thought came to mind, that I should be thankful that all of the surgeries had been for removal of benign tumors.

In 1979, I began the school year with the Rome City Schools as the Youth Employment Training Coordinator for West Rome Junior and Senior High Schools. I was back in the classroom and assisting needy students who were eligible for the C.E.T.A. program. I knew that this was not permanent, but it was a training period for me. The students were delightful and fun to be around.

Later, I was informed that I had passed the examination that would qualify me for a position with the Department of Family and Children's Services in Chattanooga County.

I began to work in Summerville, Georgia as a Child Abuse, Child Neglect Investigator with the Services Department. This was a challenge to be able to confront crisis after crisis.

One incident that remains vivid in my mind, was a day that I was informed that it would be required of me to go to a cave-like structure and retrieve a child who had been a truant from school.

The mother, part Indian, had other things on her mind. I shall never forget her name. Shirley. She was adamant about my removing her child and placing him in foster care. Her next action shocked me as she proceeded to place a hex on me and the Department.

I am not an advocate of Voo-Doo, however, there were some strange happenings to me during that period of time.

Finally in exasperation, I turned to the 23rd Psalm, only to misinterpret the writing as it stated "Shirley, goodness and mercy shall follow you all the days of your life."

I returned to work the following day to make concentrated efforts to find adequate housing for both mother and son, thereby reuniting them. Successful in achieving this task, I felt a real sense of accomplishment.

Because of my intense interest in the needy, I wrote an article for submission to the Georgia State Welfare Department Writer's contest.

To my surprise, I won the Georgia State Pen Award for 1979, and a one hundred dollar bill. My dad would have been so proud of me.

Meanwhile our music child was to enter the Music Contest for her age group at Berry College in Rome, Georgia. We were all very excited that this one had been chosen to represent Cave Spring in this endeavor.

The awaited day arrived for the competition. As always I had washed and styled her hair in Shirley Temple curls. A new dress had been purchased especially for this occasion.

This child was reminded that she should be proud of herself. I had never worn a "store bought dress" to a recital. Mommie had made all of my dresses and evening gowns. Nevertheless, I was proud of the opportunity that had been afforded to me, and wanted to instill this same pride within my children. The child had practiced long hard hours. We knew the concentrated efforts would be rewarded.

The award was a blue ribbon in two categories. Her father and I both stood tall and proud when we rose to give this, our hearing offspring a standing ovation following the performance. Even though the child was very tiny, she stood tall and proud that day.

I could visualize myself being in her place, and my parents watching and never hearing the notes or sounds of music. Her dad, like her grandparents, did not hear the strains of the grand piano as they floated through the halls that day at Berry College.

This was a special child, even at four. I was already collecting various items to place in a hope chest. A cedar chest had been purchased to protect the antique silverware that I was collecting. It also held the Cedar encased Bible Judy Cook gave on the day of the child's birth. I had dreams of one day watching this one being escorted down the aisle by her own deaf dad.

17.
FORTIETH BIRTHDAY—GRAMMY

The New Year's resolutions that I made in 1980, were those that the usual middle age woman makes.

This year I would celebrate my 40th birthday, and also my husband and I would commemorate our 25th wedding anniversary. I had looked forward to these two days with excited anticipation. How little did I know that there would be so many obstacles to hinder the happiness of both days.

One of the boys, who was now living in Mississippi, and his lovely wife announced to the family during the holidays that we would be grandparents around June. This would be our first grandchild, and we were very excited about the pending arrival. As I said, I always loved babies.

I continued to commute to Summerville daily. The stresses of my present position continued to mount. Days can be very depressing when working with people who seem to have no goal in mind except to reproduce and spend other people's money.

My birthday was nearing. I had suspected that the children would do something special since they had given their dad a surprise party on his 40th, but little did I know what they had in mind for me.

Two Sundays prior to my birthday, we attended the little country church which was located nearby. We had transferred our letter the previous fall due to factors that I will never truly understand. But I never inquired deeply. I just let the Lord intervene and He did.

Following the church services, my hubby and the younger one insisted that we ride to nearby Centre, Alabama and eat lunch. As usual, I did not object. Following the lunch, he began to ride around and look at the countryside. I usually spent Sunday afternoons reading the newspapers, clipping coupons, writing letters and preparing for the coming week at work, so therefore I was anxious to return home.

After two hours had lapsed, I insisted that we return home.

Riding down Sleepy Hollow in the springtime was again a pleasurable experience for me. I suppose it was because I knew near the dead end road was home. Our home.

Rounding the curve, I spied our house. It looked rather unusual. There were numerous automobiles surrounding the house, and parked in neighboring driveways. I began to panic. Forgetting all about my upcoming birthday, I exclaimed that something must be wrong.

When we arrived at our place, I immediately ran into the

house to see several of my friends, all of the family, and the pastor's family present. In shock, I cried out "Oh! No! Is it Mother? Is something wrong with her?"

Immediately sensing that I misinterpreted their gathering, and noticing that I was near tears, the pastor began to lead the group in singing "Happy Birthday."

What a relief! I had truly been surprised. As usual my best friends were present, and I was kidded without end regarding the number of boxes of powder that I had received as gifts. I simply adored Estee Lauder, and when asked what I needed, that was what my children had responded. I had powder to last for three years.

June of 1980 arrived. Daily I awaited the phone call that would inform us of the new birth. I had accrued two weeks of annual leave and we had already made preparations to leave immediately following the birth to go to Mississippi.

Friday the 13th, did not bring sad news, it brought joyful jubilation. The phone call came directly to me from the new father.

"Hello granny, it's a boy!" You could hear my squeals all over the D.F.C.S. office. I was now a grandmother.

Driving down the coast, my spouse and I discussed the fact that we were now grandparents. The decision was made to suggest to the children that the grandchildren now refer to us as Grammy and Granddaddy.

So thereafter, we were known as such.

The little boy, was a living doll. Upon arrival I immediately began to assist in attending to him. The parents were both exhausted, and I was more than pleased to take care of the little tyke full time. He was a good baby and our little one adored him also. At the tender age of ten, we knew this child could relinquish the position of having been the baby in the family for the past ten years. "Boog" was now the baby.

On the fifth day of our visit, my husband received a telephone call from the Superintendent of G.S.D. informing him that he would be required to return to Cave Spring in order to renew his teaching certificate for the following year.

With mixed emotions, we left the following day to return to Georgia. Another shattered dream of mine had followed the path of previous ones.

Another school year began for us. One older son was still residing at home, working at a carpet mill in Rome. Another son would be entering the eleventh grade, and the now grown baby at ten would be a fourth grader.

As for me, I had been offered a position with the State of Georgia as S.S.I. Coordinator for Northwest Georgia with offices at the District Health Office located in Rome. I coordinated services for all of the handicapped recipients of Social Security Supplemental Income who were under the age of sixteen. This involved a sixteen county area, and more than nine hundred clients.

Feeling very fortunate to have a very capable assistant, the young lady who had served as my secretary in Summerville, had been selected to become the secretary to the program. I was elated. She was so efficient, and I knew she would make my job much easier.

Traveling to the sixteen Health Departments was part of my responsibilities, therefore I was on the road a great deal of the time. It was an enjoyable line of work. The people with whom I had the opportunity to assist, made it even more rewarding. Seeing progress with these handicapped children, and knowing that I was an integral part of the process gave me a feeling of self worth that I had never known.

Enjoying my work, being a grandmother, having a house almost completed, I anxiously awaited the 25th anniversary celebration planned for November of 1980.

18.
TWENTY-FIFTH WEDDING ANNIVERSARY

Preparations were being made for the twenty-fifth anniversary celebration. Invitations and napkins had been printed, and a guest list had been compiled. We had contacted the minister who performed our initial wedding ceremony, to attend so we would renew our wedding vows. Our wedding in 1955 had not been very well planned, but it was certain that this celebration had all the preparation of any large wedding. Our planning had begun six months in advance, giving us ample time to prepare for any last minute changes.

Sunday afternoon in November 1980 would be the designated date for the anticipated joyous occasion.

Our neighbors, had graciously consented for us to use their beautiful antebellum home located just around the corner from us.

Everything was shaping up in fine form. The girls and I purchased dresses that complimented each other. The boys were helping in every way possible.

Saturday, September 28, dawned bright and beautiful. An autumn day was always the perfect time for the boys and their dad to cut firewood for the winter.

Our son, who had endured pain, was scheduled to work the evening shift at Trend Mills, therefore he could help the younger son and their dad until around 2:00 p.m. Their plans were to cut wood near home, barely a mile away.

The youngest child and I had remained at home to clean the house and prepare a meal for their return. I could hear the buzz of the chain saw from time to time, and knew that the woodcutters would be home shortly.

Suddenly, the youngster came running into the kitchen stating that Dad was driving the truck like mad and blowing the horn. Running to the front door, I thought they were just acting foolish.

Turning into the driveway at breakneck speed, the two boys were in the truck bed. Their dad signed for me to call an ambulance to meet them, and to gather towels immediately.

Panic stricken, I asked what had happened. He requested that I not go to the truck, but just call the emergency personnel to meet them enroute. He then tied a handkerchief onto the antenna of my Toyota station wagon, folding the back seat down, he picked his injured son John from the bed of the truck and laid him into the vehicle. He then asked if I would phone the neighbor to go to the wood cutting area and turn the chain saw off, and retrieve it for him.

Our youngest's son's clothing was blood soaked, and it was difficult to tell which of the boys had been injured, and how badly. I began to cry.

Immediately, I called another neighbor to ask if she would accompany me to the hospital. In addition, I asked if her husband would check on the chainsaw for us.

The child which had been left at home with me rushed to the neighbor's auto. We cried all the way to the hospital, not knowing exactly what had happened. All we knew was that there had been an injury and it was serious.

I prayed for my deaf husband and two sons as they traveled toward the emergency room located at the local hospital, twenty miles away in Rome.

Arriving at the hospital, I spied my husband looking much older than his forty-eight years.

It was at that time that I saw my youngest son. All I could see was blood everywhere. Still oblivious to what had transpired in the woods near our house.

Our injured son lay on the gurney in the Critical Care Unit. The younger son began to relate the events of the past hour.

His dad had been operating the chainsaw. He had lifted a downed limb for him to cut it in half. The hurt son, on the other side, did not realize that he was so near to the blade of the saw. As the saw blade cut through the wood, it slipped, and caught his right leg just above his knee and went straight up toward his groin area.

The chainsaw had ground through his blue jeans to the large bone in his leg. An artery had been severed. Upon seeing the blood, the younger son immediately began to apply pressure with his hands. Their dad lifted him onto the bed of the truck and they began their journey with their deaf father counting and informing the younger one as to when to release the pressure. His voice sounded like my dad's.

They met the ambulance in the middle of a small bridge on Black's Bluff Road, approximately five miles from our house. The injured son, by that time was in shock.

Having lost so much blood, he was begging the E.M.T's to amputate his leg. He was in an enormous amount of pain. With muscle, skin and, blue jean fragments embedded within the gash, the doctors worked frantically to sew up the wound. It was questionable at that time whether this son would ever be able to walk again without a limp. I continued to pray for his recovery.

The doctors completing their chore, I was then allowed to see my boy. I thanked the Lord that my second son's life had been spared. It had required more than 70 stitches to sew up his leg.

Like me this boy has never been one to give in to defeat. He used the recovery period to write letters, and compile a 25th Anniversary Book for "our day." It was second to none. Containing letters from practically every person who had ever touched our lives in any way. It was an album to become an heirloom for years to come.

The maimed son sought solace in his pain by playing with his pet bird Beretta. His bird was so unique and loved his master. Our soldier boy had acquired it while he was stationed in Arkansas during his Air Force Days. Beretta was a joy to behold.

Beretta was loved by everyone, with the exception of our youngster's Siamese cat. One day while the injured one was asleep, Beretta was no more. The feline had devoured the injured son's pride and joy.

There was sorrow on Sleepy Hollow that day. Immediately, we telephoned my husband's relative and offered to give her the cat. By nightfall, there was neither cat nor bird in our household. Two sad children spent a sleepless night within the confines of our home on Sleepy Hollow Road.

The days were flying by fast and furious prior to the ceremonial day planned in November.

Our injured boy was beginning to use crutches to move around. The tube which had been placed in his leg had now been removed, thanks to another good friend from the church, Eloise George.

A local nurse, she was real supportive at this time. She resided in Cave Spring, and would drop by the house on her way home from work each day. She would check the wound, drain the tube and place new dressing on the injured leg. The magic touch was within her hands.

Not only that, she was a fine Christian lady. Our injured one will be forever indebted to her for the kindness shown to him through this adept and skillful nurse. We feel strongly that his progress, and the results of her care staved off complications and possible infection in his leg. This reminded me of days many, many years ago when my own arms were cared for so carefully by my grandmother. I knew somewhat how my son felt. We prayed together often whenever I drove him to the doctor's office.

I was confident that he had the perseverance to walk again, waterski and do so without any detectable limp.

Meanwhile, the younger son and my spouse were painting the foyer at the neighbor's home. When she consented to allow us to use her home for the special occasion, we asked what we could do to help. She stated that the foyer was in need of a new coat of paint.

Every spare minute that the boys and their dad had, was spent on ladders painting the area surrounding the large stairway at the neighbors house located nearby. Completed, we knew it would be beautiful.

Nearing the completion of the painting, our hurt boy, cane in hand, took a brush and painted around all of the baseboards. We knew he could do it. He, like the rest of us, was a survivor.

I continued to work daily. Two close co-workers who were in the catering business in Summerville offered to donate a beautiful three tier anniversary cake, to us for the festivities. The children were elated when they learned that these ladies would be so kind to a family that had faced so many obstacles in preparations for this momentous occasion.

Another friend, Glenda Couey, the dietician at G.S.D., informed the children that she would be making a double ring chocolate "groom's cake" as a gift to us for the day.

Plans for a wonderful weekend were going smoothly. The secretary at the D.F.C.S. office, consented to help me in any way possible. We had become fast friends when I began my work in Summerville. Most important, she was one of the most dependable people that I have ever known. The day would go over without a hitch, if Gail Rush was in charge. I knew also that she would coerce the other staff members into assisting her, in order for this day to be extra special for someone she obviously admired and adored.

My dream day was nearing and I was becoming more and more excited by the minute. Our neighbor was working frantically on her house. The children, including the young one, were spending as much time as possible to insure a perfect and smooth reception of all of our friends.

Prior to the "Big Day," we were receiving cards daily. Congratulatory letters, and beautiful gifts mainly of silver were also being sent to us. They were all so beautiful. Even Dad, Mommie, and Mother would have been impressed.

Mother had chosen not to attend the celebration, for reasons unknown to me at the time. However, I tried not to let anything disappoint me.

Sunday, the designated time and date arrived.

The minister had motored in the previous day, and was prepared to assist in the ceremonial event. All of the family and, our children, were present. At the appropriate time, 2:00 p.m. our friends gathered. There was a mixture of deaf and hearing people alike in attendance. All were our dear friends.

The family convened at the top of the magnolia entwined staircase. My best friend Nancy took her seat at the piano, and several of my favorite songs were played. One of the children then sang "The Twelfth of Never," with another child accompanying, both in voice and sign language for the deaf. Our injured one leaned on the cane that was required for him to walk but his hands were still as agile as ever. It was a most beautiful sight.

My deaf husband and I then descended the staircase. All six of the children, one grandchild, two daughters-in-law, and one fiancée all stood behind us at the top of the flight of stairs near the handrails. The minister who had performed the first ceremony, the Rev. Don Reed, took his place at the foot of the stairs. Upon alighting the stairway, we stood hand in hand to renew our vows. The nimble fingers of our son leaning on his cane interpreted for all of the hearing impaired people present. Tears rolled down my cheeks. The day had finally arrived.

Following the vow renewal, we then turned, knelt and two of the children performed another duo, "The Lord's Prayer." The formalities were then completed. The festivities could begin.

Everyone was in a jovial mood. The one that I had stood by over the years, now stood with me, hands clasped, near the entrance to welcome all of those who would attend during the afternoon. My Aunt Katie King (my namesake) and Uncle Otha had driven down from Cleveland, Tennessee. I was ecstatic to see them.

The former owner of the cabin and her new husband were present as were the deaf, and others from our church.

A co-worker, had consented to make the photographs. The fall flowers in our neighbor's front yard made a beautiful setting for the family portrait. We all gathered to have a memory made. The antebellum house in the background gave the photographs a professional look. Each person's cheerful smile was depicted perfectly.

We were the epitome of a perfect family. Christians, serving the Lord, in Church and in our everyday lives, that described our family.

The past twenty-five years were very vivid in my mind. I could recall the children often telling me that I did not love them enough when I inquired where they were going, with whom, and what time they would arrive home. That love was shown when I would stand over them for two hours while they cleaned their room, a job that would have only required fifteen minutes of my time. I loved them, even when some of the children they brought home looked like creeps. It was love that made me set the alarm clock at twelve p.m. and require them to turn it off when they arrived. This was to assure that they would arrive home before the appointed hour. My love to them was to give them responsibilities at an early age, and assume the consequences of their inappropriate actions. The hardest part of showing "tough love" to my little ones was when I had to say NO and they hated me for it.

The events of the past year had not marred this joyous occasion. The fact that we would not be flying to Hawaii to continue this special time in our lives would not serve as a deterrent to my happiness that day. Maybe someday.

Once again, even through the storms of life, "Dummy's Little Girl" had seen a dream materialize.

Our young son's leg continued to heal. He began to be energetic once again. Each day when I arrived home from work, he would have a meal already prepared for us. The house would be clean, and there would be "God's Eyes" on his bed.

This multi-talented one had learned to make Spanish-Mexican "God's Eyes," to pass the time when he was a patient at Emory, therefore we always had plenty of all sizes of wooden rods and colorful yarn at his disposal.

He could create some of the most beautiful wall hangings

that I had ever seen. We knew he was definitely on the road to recovery.

The Carpet Mill announced they were closing the Rome Plant. This meant that our boy would be required to seek other employment. He was not too happy about the idea, but we knew he would persevere.

The holidays came and we gathered as a family unit as always. Little did I know when I made my New Year resolutions at that time what '81 would hold in store.

My husband had become known in deaf circles as a good leader. He was now being recognized for his accomplishments. We were offered the opportunity to become part-time missionaries to the deaf at a neighboring school for the deaf in Alabama. Talladega was a two hour drive from Cave Spring. Once a month, he and I would motor to the antiquated town where my dad had begun his formal education in the twenties. Many of the former buildings were still standing having been renovated over the years to keep them in good repair.

It was my responsibility to lead the congregation of deaf students in singing choruses, prior to the sermon. My husband the minister would then conduct the services in sign language, and I interpreted for those in attendance who could not read his signs. It came natural, because I had performed this gesture for him for more than twenty-five years now.

We loved the deaf children. Not only did we attend the services, often we would drive over a day early in order to mingle with them on Saturdays. Basketball and football games were usually on the agenda for Saturdays, so therefore we enjoyed attending those functions also.

The Superintendent of both the school for the deaf and blind, was a most generous man. He was a fine Christian man and loved the deaf. Surprisingly enough, he knew sign language also.

A local philanthropist was always present. He loved the deaf children and was very instrumental in securing a new chapel in which the children could worship. It was a place of beauty. We enjoyed ministering in such a lovely place dedicated to the Lord.

Our ministry continued on other weekends at the local community church where several deaf people were in attendance.

Nancy Barker and I shared interpreting responsibilities there. These were good times for us.

In the spring of '81, the children began to notice that I experienced difficulty in hearing. I had detected it several months prior to their mentioning it, however I was afraid to mention the problems that I was experiencing. I was losing my hearing, and the fear of deafness overwhelmed me.

Several months passed before I finally mustered enough courage to go to the Eye-Ear-Nose-specialist. He recommended an audiological examination.

The results were devastating to me. I was fitted with hearing aids. My hearing was declining at a very fast rate, and the possibilities of my becoming totally deaf within five years were extremely high. I cried. I prayed. I begged God to remove this obstacle. Wearing the hearing aids made me extremely nervous. I admit, I could hear better, but the quality of hearing was very poor.

I felt certain that I would never be able to hear well enough to interpret a sermon, a Gospel singing, a wedding, a funeral or any other function, ever again. I looked on my hearing aids as "sticks in the mud." I had joined the world of the "hearing impaired." I was now a consumer of interpreting services, not a provider. It was maddening.

My husband had received another state award and was being nominated for Handicapped Georgian of the Year. The children were very excited, because this would mean our family would gather once again to pay tribute to the leader of the family for his accomplishments.

One day during that spring a letter arrived from our deaf son Earl, who was still in attendance at Gallaudet College in Washington, D.C.

He was informing us that he had finally completed his requirements for a degree after thirteen years of trudging along.

He was now a candidate for graduation from the prestigious college. He would now have the distinction of being the first child to receive a college diploma.

Plans were made for us to travel to Washington. The ceremonies were planned to be held in the National Shrine. Excitement began to grow on Sleepy Hollow Road. We would make the trip.

Gallaudet College had made plans for all of the parents who were in attendance for their respective children's graduation. Tours, parties, brunches, cook-outs and housing was afforded to all of us. We were having a great time.

The son who had endured hardships also, with his head held high, marched across the stage of the beautiful and majestic National Shrine to receive his long awaited "sheep-skin." Near the center of the auditorium sat a family who had adopted him as their own child. We all applauded and cried simultaneously. Knowing how far he had come, the hurdles that he had to stride, the obstacles that he had to overcome and the mountains that he had to climb in order to reach this day, were fresh in my mind.

He, like the other deaf members of my family had endured. This son had been deafened at age three by spinal meningitis. The results of the elevated temperature had caused the nerves extending from his ears to his brain to be permanently damaged causing total deafness.

Again I was reminded of my own dad's plight.

His mother had passed away earlier when he was nine years of age. She had left four small children to be cared for. His father, had done the best that he could with all of them.

When he was seventeen, his father died suddenly of a heart attack. He was now orphaned, deaf, homeless but very intelligent.

We entered the picture shortly thereafter. He remained a student at M.S.D., the same school that my parents, and husband had attended.

This young deaf man was a star student. A known bookworm, he loved to read anything that he could get his hands on.

He was also an avid sportsman and enjoyed the outdoors. An all-round young man, we knew he would do well. He graduated as Valedictorian of his class at my parents' and his adopted dad's school.

That day at "Gally" as he represented our family, his family, and his deceased parents, he stood as an example of what deafened individuals can and do accomplish.

He was no "dummy" and never would be.

The injured one's leg was improving nicely. In fact, he had

volunteered to "dance in the marathon" at Floyd Junior College. The proceeds from the dance would be designated for the local cancer society. Stubborn, he was going to make an attempt to win the contest.

Six months had lapsed since that autumn day in the woods near our home on Sleepy Hollow where his leg was mauled by the chainsaw. Nevertheless, he was going to try to do his best.

The designated day arrived. Carefully he had chosen a dancing partner. The marathon began with approximately 55 couples on the floor. The youngest, their dad, and I remained there to boost his spirits and to see if he could endure the pressure and the pain of dancing on his injured leg.

Surprisingly enough, seventy-eight hours later, he and his partner were the only couple remaining on the dance floor. They had won the marathon, a trophy and a nice newspaper article handing out accolades for their accomplishment.

Just like my dad and his dad, he had persevered once again.

Following the contest, later during the week, he decided to visit another brother to seek employment. Having arrived in Mississippi, he discovered that seeking employment there was just as difficult as it was in Georgia.

However, he landed a job on a supply boat at Bayou LaBatre, Alabama, near Mobile. With an injured leg, he now had to acquire "sea legs." This he did very well. Getting a tan and enjoying his job, he was satisfied with his work. The leg was fine. John was on his way now!

Later that year, I was informed that the S.S.I. position would not be renewed for the following year. I would be transferring to the Mental Health Office in another city. The commute would be approximately sixty four miles a day.

Disappointed, I accepted the news as gracefully as possible. I had enjoyed the position, but understood about Federal grants and funding.

My husband, had been given the honor of opening the Georgia State Senate in prayer at the Georgia State Capitol in Atlanta, Georgia. Having been named Minister for the Day, by a local senator, he was the first deaf minister to ever be awarded this opportunity. Several of our friends accompanied us to the Senate gallery.

As I stood beside him, with microphone in hand, he led the

state leaders in prayer while closing it with the poem that I had penned, "The Deaf Christian's Prayer." There was not a dry eye in the house. I felt proud, so very proud that day as official photographs were made of our family and friends with state officials.

I even went so far as to go by the governor's office, and inquire of the secretary, if a photograph could be made of our entourage with the governor himself.

On a previous occasion, it had been my pleasure to be chosen to serve as the official interpreter for him. He remembered me, and honored the request.

Good humoredly, the kids had said it would not surprise them if I invited him over for dinner.

A few days later I received a letter from the Mississippi School for the Deaf announcing my mother's retirement.

Mother had reached the age of retirement, and was not doing well health-wise. Several years previously she had suffered from a detached retina, requiring surgery. I went there and spent a week with her while she was in the hospital.

She also had problems with her feet and legs swelling. The concrete floors were not advantageous to her problem, therefore the doctors recommended that she retire. Her plans were to reside with Bubba until there was a vacancy at the Methodist Retirement Center in Tupelo.

I planned to go to her retirement party scheduled for a Thursday.

Driving out to the local airport, I inquired of the owners if there was an available pilot who would be willing to fly me to Jackson for the day.

They directed me to one of their local pilots who had just procured a new airplane. It had never been in the air for a long trip, and was a picture of beauty. He agreed to transport me and two other family members for only $100.00, for the entire day.

I called Nancy to convey this information to my deaf husband. We would soon be making a selection as to which child would accompany us. Making the downpayment, I left fully expecting to leave the following Thursday morning at 7:00 a.m.

It was decided that our angel son would be the one accompanying us on the journey, because the other children had seen their grandmother more recently than he.

Arriving at home, my friend telephoned to tell me that she did not feel good about the plane trip. I just laughed and said she was just joshing. I even teased her about being jealous for not having been selected to go along for the ride.

"Oh! But no!" she exclaimed. Apparently she did not cherish the idea of a plane ride to Mississippi, nor any other place for that matter. I had not been feeling well for several weeks. While driving to work early Thursday morning, I began to experience severe stomach pains. By the time I had arrived at work the excruciating pain had accelerated. I was on the verge of collapse at any minute.

Upon entering the building at the office, I went immediately to the Ladies' Room. There, I passed out.

The next thing I recall was lying on a gurney in the emergency room in the local hospital. The attending physician took X-rays and recommended that I be transferred immediately to the hospital in Rome.

The staff at the office telephoned my husband's place of work, and asked if Nancy could convey the message to him. She did and he was soon on his way.

At the hospital, it was discovered that I had a mass within my abdominal cavity. I began to pray.

I was only 42 at the time, and felt that I had not completed my mission here on earth. A kind nurse came to comfort me. She prayed with me and gave me comfort that I needed at that time. Surgery was planned for seven o'clock the following morning.

My room was being filled with flowers even as I was wheeled out toward the Operating Room. I made a request of my attending physician that he please inform my husband of any developments. He should not be kept in the dark, even though he was deaf. I also wanted to be kept informed. I was prepared for the worst, but prayed for the best.

I remained in surgery for more than five hours. The doctors were amazed at what they had discovered when they made the incision. Two large tumors lay inside my stomach. One the size of a cantaloupe, and the other the size of a grapefruit. They were both attached to the ovaries. One had ruptured, and bled prior to the surgical procedure. That had been the source of my intense pain.

A portion of each ovary was removed in addition to the tumors. It was felt that if they were benign, then I should keep as much of the hormone producing ovaries as long as possible.

The lab results were a definite answer to my prayer. Both tumors were benign, with no malignancy whatsoever. I thanked the Lord for His watchful care that night as I lay in my hospital bed.

During the night I awoke in a medicated induced daze and summoned the nurse on duty. When she stepped inside the room, I inquired of her as to whether I had bore another son, or daughter. Laughingly she said, neither, that I been through a surgical procedure and everything was fine. My spouse lay on a cot near my bed with the light cord attached to his arm where I could reach it. He never stirred because he did not hear the nurse enter the room. He remained asleep and slept throughout the night, because I had not turned on the light. This is how he would have been awakened.

Mother had her retirement party without any of us present. I had ordered her a dozen roses to let her know that we cared. She then left Jackson to make Tupelo her home.

The following Sunday, Nancy came for a visit. For some unknown reason the nurses, children and even my husband had not permitted me to read the local newspaper that day. I was becoming more and more agitated by the hour.

When she entered the room, she said, "Doris, I just wanted you to know that the children called me and requested that I come and visit you." Then she handed me the newspaper. On the front page was the picture of the new airplane embedded into the side of a barn located in a town nearby. The pilot and his wife had been on a flight from the airport where I had been on Monday, and had crashed.

Fortunately, the pilot survived, but his wife had been killed instantly.

My dear trusted friend had to say no more. We just prayed and thanked the Lord that our family had not been on that plane.

One week later, I returned home to recuperate from the surgery. I would be away from my work for six weeks, then would return to a new position in Cedartown.

Six weeks later, I arrived at my new position in Cedartown, only seventeen miles away. My new responsibilities were to be in charge of the new Day Treatment program for the Mental Health Office located in the heart of town.

My office was located in a large two-story house painted pea green. We immediately dubbed it "The Best Little Greenhouse in Polk County."

We averaged serving twenty clients daily from the Cedartown and Rockmart area. The people in attendance were like one large family. Each had their own set of problems, but we all shared each others joys and sorrows.

The daily ride to pick them up in the van was an unusual experience. They all enjoyed the ride, and we would sing as we rode along. It reminded me of the days when my children were small and we would travel. The time passed quickly that way.

The Center was instrumental in securing a piano, so naturally, we had a songfest each afternoon following lunch. My how those people could sing. They could lift the rafters of that little green house.

Holidays were special times also, but they were also depressing for those who had emotional problems. This was the hardest part of my job to deal with them when they were depressed.

The following year, I was rushed to the hospital, with severe abdominal pains. Not fully understanding what could be the cause this time, it was discovered that the left ovary had developed a type of endometriosis. Another surgical procedure was performed and the ovary was removed. A portion of the other one was also removed, so all that was left was a tiny piece that would produce enough hormones to keep the hormonal balance equalized.

Because of my short stature, and the congenital pituitary problem, it was important that I retain as much as possible of the natural hormone within my body.

Because I was so short, and it was very noticeable, children would often stand behind me and measure their own height to mine. Invariably, they would question if I was a midget or a dwarf. My classic response was "neither, I am a mixture—I am a digit, one of a kind."

My dad had endured the same stares as I had over the years, and it was apparent that some of my other children had inherited the same genes. The trait was one that does not cause one to have problems associated with dwarfism, but does create other medical problems.

It was evident that I was beginning to exemplify some of these as I grew older. Back pain and leg cramps were a constant companion. Also the water retention and edema did not help matters.

Following the doctors orders as closely as I could, I made attempts to reduce my ever increasing weight, but it was to no avail.

It seemed that I would not recover from one surgical procedure, before I was going back under the knife again.

The year, 1986, I awoke one night with severe pain in my right side. The last piece of ovary would have to be removed, I was certain.

Three days later, I had no more ovaries and hopefully that was the end of any more surgery for me. Dr. Sunay removed a football sized tumor this time. The doctors and nurses began to tease me whenever I returned for more surgery. They said it would have been simpler to place a zipper on my tummy, then whenever I had a problem, they could just unzip me.

My husband had received more awards. Among those were the Floyd County Handicapped Citizen of the Year, The Mary Huckaby Award. The Heart of the Community Award, and the Georgia Association of the Deaf Special Award. We had made one room into a shrine to his honor.

His football helmet, inscribed with the dates of M.S.D.'s winning team hung in the den along with his trophy. Pictures of the family were placed on every wall within our home on Sleepy Hollow Road.

We began to spend more time in Mississippi. We had purchased a Holiday Travel Trailer, and had placed it on the property that my husband had inherited from his parents.

Meanwhile, our son John had moved to Mississippi and was now employed at Cooper Tire Company in Tupelo. His dream was to own the old homeplace.

A year later, he realized his dream, and purchased the old farmhouse. His plans were to raise and train Tennessee Walking Horses.

We spent holidays there, and I would prepare large meals and invite friends and relatives there. We loved the farm. It brought back many happy memories for all of us.

My husband had been nominated to be inducted into the Mississippi School for the Deaf Hall of Fame.

The selection committee contacted me, and I wrote his bibliography and mailed it immediately. We were certain that he would win the coveted award.

If he was selected as a recipient, it would be a culmination of the Award of all Awards. It was considered similar to the movie industries "Oscar."

We spent Christmas and New Year's Day at John's in Mississippi, in 1988.

Little did I know what would be in store for me for the coming year. As always, I made New Year's resolutions that I could never seem to keep.

19.
THE THIRTIETH YEAR TENT MAKERS (MORE GRANDBABIES)

I began to experience severe health problems. Debilitating headaches were a common occurrence, accompanied by fluid retention within my body.

My weight reached an all time high of over 200 pounds. My feet were often so swollen, it was difficult for me to wear shoes. Regardless of the concentrated efforts that I made, it was still difficult for me to lose any weight.

Early in February of 1989, I had a severe bout with the flu. My body was encased in pain and filled with fluid.

Years earlier, I had been diagnosed as having a mitral valve prolapse in my heart. It is not an unusual occurrence, as 80% of the women today, have the same problem. It is more an inconvenience than a handicapping condition. Antibiotics must be taken prior to dental or surgical procedures to ward off infection.

My body had retained so much fluid, that I was experiencing difficulty in sleeping at night. I often felt that I would literally drown in my own body fluids.

I awoke during the early morning hour of February 3rd. I had a splitting headache, and the shooting pains felt as if a bullet had punctured my brain.

Not bothering to awaken anyone, I walked from the bedroom to the den area. The wood heater was still warm, and I placed a piece of firewood within the heater. As I bent to close the heater door, I began to feel a numbness in my left leg, arm and face.

Stumbling to the couch, I made attempts to awaken one of the children who was sleeping in the bedroom nearby. I could feel my eyes and mouth drooping. I rubbed my shoulder and left side with my right hand. I tried to talk, but could only utter guttural sounds.

I began to choke, my airway had been obstructed by my tongue. Feeling a sense of helplessness, I began to make grunting sounds. My child still did not respond. In a last attempt to arouse her and gain her attention, I tossed a throw pillow onto the coffee table nearby.

From the bedroom I heard a voice. I made more sounds. Realizing that something was amiss, she came into the den.

She knew that I had been ill with the flu, and it was not unusual for me to sleep on the couch, she glanced at me and began to return to her bedroom. I made one last attempt to gain her attention. This time she responded.

Upon detecting that my face was limp and the obstruction of my breathing, she immediately began to administer C.P.R. procedures. After placing a pillow behind my neck to hold my head in place, she ran immediately to the back bedroom to retrieve her dad.

Her actions were quick, precise and skillful. She dialed the telephone for the emergency personnel and continued to work with my limp body.

When the ambulance arrived, I was taken immediately to the trauma unit at Redmond Park Hospital. I already knew that I had suffered a stroke, but how serious, I did not know.

The neurologist was at another hospital, however, he arrived shortly after the E.M.T.'s had placed me on the Emergency

Room gurney. A spinal tap was performed immediately, and C.A.T. scans ordered. My daughter continued to work with my withered hand and leg. I had always instructed them to massage the affected area, in case I did suffer a stroke. I had also told them to talk to me or play music if I ever lapsed into a coma.

An arteriogram was performed, and diuretic intravenous fluids were being administered.

The children were called, and they all came immediately. John arrived from Mississippi around noon.

I remained in the hospital for several days, then was released to return home. I knew that the rehabilitation process would be long and hard, but I was determined not to be crippled.

Daily, I would make efforts to walk. Dragging my left leg, I would try to go outside. The front porch was as far as I could go for several weeks. The atrophy in my left hand had caused it to become drawn.

I would look at my prized organ and piano and cry wondering if I would ever have the ability to move my fingers across the keys again.

My mind would race back to the days when Mommie had prayed so hard for my "little hands." I would recall the words that she had spoken to me from the Bible. "Let not your hands be weak for they shall be rewarded." I prayed a simple prayer. "Let my hands move for the Lord and His glory."

After two months and hours of therapy, I began to make efforts to walk outside. With much effort, I could walk the short distance to the mailbox and back in thirty minutes. Following my walk, I would be exhausted and would cry. I was very depressed.

Teena Cagle, one of my co-workers would call me on a daily basis and encourage me. She had become one of my best friends and support system since I had been stricken.

Nancy Barker, and Bro. Bailey called me often, as did the children.

Time passed so slowly. I had been so accustomed to a fast pace in life, that the confinement had been similar to a train traveling at one hundred miles an hour, hitting a brick wall and being derailed.

Life for me was at a complete standstill.

My speech began to return, along with some of the feeling in my face. I was compelled to drink liquids with the aid of a straw. Eating was a chore because I seemed to drop most of my food on my clothing. Life became useless to me at times. However, through the encouragement of everyone, I knew I had to persevere.

I had not been grocery shopping for three months. My husband insisted that I go, and ride the little cart provided for handicapped individuals. Not wanting to disappoint him, I consented to do this.

I felt so helpless and humiliated when the shoppers would stare at me. I did not want to be handicapped. I wanted to walk. I knew that with God's help, I would accomplish it one day.

20.
THE THIRTY-FIFTH YEAR, MISSIONARIES AND TRAVELING

Since Mother's retirement, I had established a Scholarship Fund in honor of Mother, Dad, and my husband at the Mississippi School for the Deaf. Each year, I had contributed $100.00 to the most deserving Vocational Student in the graduating class.

I wanted to attend the graduation this year. That was a goal that I had established for myself. I began to walk more and exercise my hand in warm water for hours. I knew that it could be done if I persisted.

We had invited Mr. and Mrs. Dillard to accompany us on the trip to Jackson. We were looking forward to the trip.

The speech that I had prepared, would require me to use sign language and speech simultaneously. I practiced for hours in front of the bedroom mirror. With determination, I knew that it could be done. With God's help I knew that I could perform flawlessly.

We made the trip to M.S.D. I made the presentation. My husband videotaped it with our new camcorder. Hardly a limp could be detected in my walk. My speech was slurred at times, and my hands were not as agile as before, but I was successful in my goal.

My spouse of thirty-four years had been named to the Mississippi School for the Deaf Hall of Fame. We were delighted that we would be attending the ceremonies on the Gulf Coast.

Too, we would be going on a cruise following the festivities. I was all excited. Dad and Mommie would have been so proud. The trip to Hawaii did not seem so important now.

I was walking much better. The road to full recovery would be long and hard, but I had traveled that pathway before and knew what would be required of me.

The Lord would have to be near me. A combination of faith and stamina would be the only solution to gaining full use of all of my faculties.

The children assisted me in preparing a poster for display at the H.O.F. Banquet. John would interpret for his Dad, and another child would assist. They were both skilled interpreters.

Another close friend of ours, would be receiving a similar award to my husband's. It would be a wonderful occasion for all of us. I knew many happy memories would be made while we were there celebrating this momentous occasion for the father of my children.

The cruise was both beautiful and relaxing. All of our friends were aboard, and most of them were deaf. We were having the time of our life. I did not want it to end. I was in a fantasy land and it felt good.

The only sad part, was that my mother and dad were not present to share in such a happy occasion. They would have enjoyed every minute of the activities, and especially mingling with their deaf peers.

As we watched the dolphins play in the international waters of the Gulf of Mexico, I realized that another dream had come true.

"Dummy's Little Girl," was among friends. The world of the deaf was her whole life and always would be. That's all she had ever known.

Nettleton High School Alumni was planning a combination class reunion and honor to former coach. Jack Carlisle.

Coach Carlisle would be inducted into the Mississippi High School Hall of Fame within the next few months.

I had been invited to attend.

Ironically, my husband did not want to accompany me to "my" festivities. However, I insisted that he do so. He felt so out of place among my hearing peers. I could understand, but as my spouse, I would be uncomfortable without him.

Reluctantly, he went along, and captured precious moments for me on the camcorder.

Bubba was one of the key speakers. Dad would have been so proud of him had he been present to see his little boy, now a grown man standing proud and tall give his accolades to the man who gave him so much guidance in his athletic endeavors.

Bubba, unlike me, was tall. Standing almost six feet, he continued to "look like a football player."

His wife Kaye, two children, Amanda and Justin accompanied him. He had succeeded in life and held a very prominent position with the Vocational Rehabilitation Department in the State of Mississippi.

I can still hear Dad's voice ringing in my ears as he would yell and clap for his son as his watchful eye noted every mistake he made on the playing field.

My life-long dream was to have an official High School Diploma from Nettleton High School. I was the only individual in my family who did not have that official document. It would be something to cherish. So, I just settled for the G.E.D., feeling always it was second best.

I continued to walk with a limp, and the atrophy in my left hand was still detectable. My face still felt numb, as if I had been administered a permanent shot of novocaine.

During the Thanksgiving holidays, it was decided that we would gather at the Partridge restaurant and have dinner. The children did not feel that I was strong enough to handle meal preparation for the large family. I consented.

I also made plans for a photographer to be present to take pictures of all of us. Mother would be there, and I just felt the need to have some good photographs of all the family.

Mother had not been well, and plans were for her to have a battery of tests around the end of the year. She, like me, had gained an enormous amount of weight, and also the problem of fluid retention.

I had consented to accompany her to the hospital for these tests, in the latter part of the following January.

The New Year was celebrated at John's place in New Albany. As usual, the same New Year's resolutions were made. Too, as always I would be making resolutions and not seeming to keep them. However, little did I know what a chaotic year I would spend in 1990. It would be comparable to none that I had ever lived in my entire fifty years.

I would be celebrating my fiftieth birthday and hoping for a great day to remember for years to come. I had survived in a deaf world for one half of a century. In the mind's eye, that is quite a long period of time.

The annual Mason-Dixon Basketball tournaments for the deaf were being held in Alabama and Georgia. This would be the first time that I had missed seeing the tourney in a number of years.

But mother was a priority, and I felt compelled to help her as much as possible. She had been scheduled to have the examinations performed at that time, therefore I felt compelled to relinquish my own desires to assist in interpreting for her.

During the process of her surgical procedure, the doctor administered some Sodium Pentothal, and my mother revealed some very frightening things regarding my husband. I could not believe them, but just hid them in my heart to save for another day if need be.

Our youngest child would soon be celebrating her twenty-first birthday and would be moving out of the house to her own apartment. She was excited about her move. In addition I sensed wedding bells would ring in the near future and she would ride down Sleepy Hollow in a horse-drawn carriage and be wed in the gazebo. One of our dreams.

21.
THE BEGINNING OF THE END: MY 50TH BIRTHDAY

My 50th birthday would arrive on March 29th, as usual. I had decorated the solarium, hoping the children would at least come by or call me.

The day of my birth arrived. One of my children drove to my office and presented me with the surprise of my life. It was a leather encased official High School Diploma from Nettleton, Mississippi. I cried tears of joy. I was now a bona-fide graduate of Nettleton, High School.

With much effort, phone calls, and planning, this child who wanted to surprise a mother had pulled off the impossible. It was a gift second to none. One that no amount of money could have purchased to make one mother happy at a turning point in her life.

I drove to G.S.D. to meet my spouse, as I hoped he would take me out for dinner on this special occasion. He had purchased some mylar balloons and they were in one of our vehicles parked in the driveway at the G.S.D. campus. I noticed them and knew he would be planning something especially nice for me that day.

Stepping inside the automobile, I spied a card and a letter. It was not addressed to me. It was to be mailed to someone else. Someone whom I had been suspecting was trying to destroy our marriage.

My husband of thirty-five years had been acting suspicious lately; but I did not know the reason. Someone had informed me of some vicious rumors, none of which I would believe. This man, the epitome of fatherhood, manhood, and a wonderful husband was my Knight in Shining Armor. My world that I had built into an empire, began to fall. Of all days, my 50th birthday. I wanted to commit suicide.

The man who had shared my life for thirty-five years arrived on Sleepy Hollow Road, as planned. The children arrived one by one. We all convened in the bedroom. Unexpectedly, a sad look came over his face and he made his announcement to all of them, including me.

He did not want a short, fat wife anymore. His desire was to be free to date other women. His choice was for younger women and a motorcycle, a Gold Wing. That was his dream.

He also stated that he had never loved me, that he married me only because of my dad and the tragedy. He wanted to leave.

He requested that I leave and give him thirty minutes to gather his clothing. I honored his request. He then drove off in his auto.

Later, as I returned to an empty house, his silver wedding band lay on the table in the foyer. I knew that he was gone. This was for good.

We had never been separated in our thirty-five years of marriage. He had left me alone numerous summers, to stay in Mississippi on the farm, but I had always managed to spend as many weekends there as possible. This was by mutual agreement.

He had meant business when he left. Where he was planning to go, I did not know.

I prayed for guidance. My heart ached and I cried. I could not live this kind of existence any more. I was alone and lonely.

My Bible lay beside the bed, and I began to read it, searching for some solace. The daily readings in the book "Streams in the Desert," left me with little comfort.

I telephoned one of my friends. Sobbing, I could hardly speak. She tried to comfort me as she told me not to worry, he would return. She felt he was only going through mid-life crisis and this was a natural phenomena with men. This kind of behavior was indicative of someone who was discontent. I cried and prayed some more.

Days passed without my hearing from him. To my surprise, the children had abandoned me also. This I could not understand. I had been guilty of nothing, and could not understand their behavior, unless they knew something that I did not know.

I became depressed immediately. Each day, as I drove down Sleepy Hollow Road to my work, I cried all the way to work. I cried at work and I cried at home. That was all that I seemed to do was cry.

Each evening when I arrived at home, I would call one friend then another. I found solace in talking to both of them. They were my mainstay at that time. God knew that I needed them desperately.

I tried to control my emotions, but nothing seemed to work. I felt totally addicted to this man who had replaced my dad in my life. I could not live without him. He had been the perfect husband, the perfect father, and the perfect partner in everything, I thought.

Implementing efforts to maintain some normalcy to my life,

I tried to continue in the church where our family had held membership for more than ten years. The memories were too painful. I felt so worthless, unneeded, unwanted and unloved.

One Sunday, following Sunday school, I decided to end it all. I drove to Buchanan, past Cedartown, checked into a motel, and took eight pills to put me to sleep forever.

This was similar to the summer of 1955. I could not go on without someone to be there when I needed him. Just wanting to go on to Heaven, I fell asleep in the motel room.

Two hours later, I awoke, uncertain as to where I was, and experiencing difficulty in breathing. I knew that my lungs were on the verge of ceasing to function if I did not seek help.

Remembering nothing, I managed to get in my new Toyota Camry, drive the thirty or so miles back to Sleepy Hollow, and call one of my friends. She had been ill, but sensing the seriousness of the situation, called another friend nearby.

Shortly afterward, the friend arrived. I looked a mess. Instructing me to put on my clothing, she took me to the hospital.

I continued to tell her to direct me to the button to Heaven and I would push it. I did not want to live anymore. She continued to tell me, that she did not know where the button was, but that the Lord was not finished with me yet and just hang in there. "Everything will be all right," she said. "You'll make it. You are a survivor."

I was admitted to the hospital for several days, under psychiatric care. A basket-case, I could not seem to pull it together.

The fifth day, the psychiatrist entered my room, told me to gather my clothing, pull myself together and go home. I trusted him, and knew there must be a reason for this kind of behavior on his behalf.

No one was available to take me home. The children all refused to provide any transportation. I had to resort to telephoning one of my very best friends, at work.

Promptly, she arrived to take me home. She had a "Peace Plant" in her car and she gave it to me to keep. She encouraged me to take solace in the plant and nourish it as I should my own body.

When we arrived at Sleepy Hollow, my automobile was not in the driveway. Shortly thereafter, the man who was still my husband arrived driving my car. He said he was concerned. All of the trust that I had built in him over the years was now void in my life. I could not accept his sympathy.

With tears in his eyes, he said he was filing for a divorce. I said nothing. There was nothing to say. It was his choice and if that would make him happy, then I would accept it.

I entered the house to cry some more. I knew for certain that if there would be an attempted suicide again, it would not be via pills. It was too painful.

The days began to pass by, oh so slowly. I refused to eat. I slept very little, and was in a state of deep grief.

To use an analogy, I felt as if I had been a tree, with an axe implanted within its trunk, and I was bleeding within. If someone would just remove the axe, the gash would be left, but the pain would go away.

However, the pain did not subside. I began to lose weight rapidly and I also began to lose my hair. Friends and neighbors became concerned. I was not acting in a normal fashion.

Sleepy Hollow was not the same place. The serene solitude that I had enjoyed over the years no longer existed.

The laughter of children echoed through the walls of my abode. Their pictures, including those of my talented husband surrounded me. His clothing remained in the closet for me to see each time I entered it. Each night I would place one of his tee-shirts, with a few drops of his favorite cologne, "Old Spice" on it. Then I would place the shirt on the pillow that he once slept on. Afterward, I would cry myself to sleep.

I hated to get up in the morning to go to work. I wrote letters. I walked the floor.

One of the most memorable cards that I received came from his sister. She included a quotation from Peter DeWise, "We are placed on this earth, not to see through others, but to see others through." It was signed, "Love, Nell."

Life was too complicated for me to face alone. It was too lonely on Sleepy Hollow Road.

22.
HIM

The man that I had once trusted with my entire life left Cave Spring to go to Mississippi for the summer. He had spent the three previous summers there on the farm with our son. He had not filed for a divorce. I was left to manage alone.

By this time, I had lost approximately forty pounds, and did not look the picture of health. I was a pitiful sight.

My Aunt Katie and Uncle Otha, in Cleveland, Tennessee, encouraged me to visit them. The visit was like a shot in the arm.

My aunt and uncle along with their son, Joe, encouraged me to get on with my life and cease my grieving. They told me I had too much to live for, and should be proud of what I had accomplished over the years, and accept this as another chapter in my life. A change that I must accept.

Revived by the visit, I returned with new vim and vigor. This was when "HIM" entered my life.

"HIM" was not like BoBo, he was not an imaginary playmate, he was for real. We had bumped into each other at one of the shopping centers in Rome. We sat on a bench outside of the store and talked for three hours. I listened closely to every word that he had to say. "HIM" was special.

"HIM" encouraged me to begin an exercise program. He also gave me instructions regarding my health. I listened. We agreed to meet again, at another time and another place.

Later, we met again. This time he encouraged me to set some goals and to look forward to some dreams.

I confessed that I had a fear of heights and of water. He offered to pay for flying and swimming lessons. I accepted readily.

The last words that I had told my husband as he was leaving were that I had never dated another man, and that I was afraid of men. The world, I knew, was filled with unscrupulous people. I needed to be cautious.

"HIM" agreed to meet me at another site. Each time we would talk for hours. He began to aid in building some self-esteem within myself. Each time we met, he would greet me with the words, "You beautiful doll, you tiny little beautiful doll." He made me feel worthwhile. I loved it.

"HIM" was married. I was cautious and so was he. We had known each other through mutual friends many years previously. His wife was ill and he was very devoted to her. I knew it. I could never let myself fall in love with "HIM." He would only serve as a mentor. A platonic relationship, was all that I could have with this man.

"HIM" encouraged me on another occasion to get involved in some activity that would bring me pleasure. I had loved to dance as a young girl, and had not danced in quite a while. However, I wanted to maintain my dignity and always remain a lady. I did not want to frequent any bars, or dives where my presence would be misinterpreted.

"HIM" agreed with me. We would talk on the telephone for hours. His voice was so consoling. I could only wish that he was available but I dared not make mention of any such thing. We were very secretive and careful in our contacts. If the gossip-mongers of Cave Spring suspected that I was doing this, they would have a hey-day.

23.
"THE VISION"

I continued to pray. My prayer was that the Lord would send the man I loved, my dad or my mommie back to me. I prayed faithfully each night. I prayed and believed.

One night, following a very strenuous day at work, I fell asleep almost immediately upon retirement. It was the middle of June. I had a very vivid dream. It was definitely a vision, sent from the Lord.

Three men stood at the foot of my bed. I was startled! The men on each side held the arms of the man in the middle. I reached to turn on my touch-lamp. I was instructed by the middle man not to do so. His voice was deep, and precise. He informed me that I should not beg and pray for the Lord to send my husband back, but to begin thanking Jesus that my prayer had been answered. My prayer had been heard. There was a man for me, and he would come in due season. I begged him to give me a name. He said that he could not do that. I insisted and would not let them leave until he consented. His words were that he would give me a name, but it was not the right one. I must be diligent and continue to pray, but my prayer should be one of thanksgiving, not of requesting.

The trio disappeared as rapidly as they appeared. I turned on my light and picked up the telephone. I dialed the number of dial-a-prayer as I did approximately ten times daily. The scripture was appropriate.

24.
THE SUMMER OF '90

I could hardly wait until morning to telephone my prayer partner. It was summer time and she was not in school so therefore I knew she would be sleeping in. At nine I could wait no longer. I related my dream, and asked her if she believed in visions. Her reply was "Oh, but yes!" I then asked her if she knew anyone by the name of "Chuck." that was the name the man had given me.

She related a few possibilities, and I decided to give one of them a call.

I did call one. He was a fine Christian man, and had lost his wife a few years earlier. We talked often. I would drive by and chat with him on occasions. Somehow, I did not feel that this was the person in my vision, because his voice was not the same. I would recognize the voice anywhere. I knew that I would.

Late in June, while at the Post Office, I met an old friend. He, not knowing that I was now alone, tried to console me. Dennis Mason, the former mayor of Cave Spring, had taught my only daughter how to waterski.

His wife, Beth was in Saudi Arabia on a nursing assignment. Dennis' stepdaughter, who had been the same age as my daughter was still at home. She had married, and was expecting her first child. I immediately became a surrogate mother to her. I enjoyed her company, and she filled a void in my life.

When I mentioned to Dennis that "HIM" had suggested dancing as therapy, he recommended the American Legion.

I knew no one who was a member of the Legion, so therefore that was out of the picture for now.

Another visit was made to Aunt Katie's and Uncle Otha's. I

told them about my vision. I related the dream to everyone with whom I came in contact. I was searching diligently for "Chuck." Aunt Katie was confident that if I ever saw him, that I would recognize him immediately. She had faith in me and believed my dream.

I visited other relatives, and met other men. Everywhere I went, they had someone for me to meet. Some were nice, some not so nice, others sticks in the mud, and a few who were too egotistical for me.

One man in particular that I met, was very wealthy. He, however had never really "buried his wife." I enjoyed the times spent with him, our life was a continuous party. It appeared that I was having my own mid-life crisis. I was cautious as not to mar my testimony. To maintain my lady-like demeanor was my ultimate goal.

Traveling all over the south, visiting long lost relatives and friends, filled many of my lonely hours. My friend would fly his lear jet to a nearby airport, and have a limo to pick me up on Sleepy Hollow.

I was even invited to join a group on a cruise to Cancun. I was having a wonderful time, other than suffering an awful touch of "Montezuma's Revenge."

On our return, we were approximately twenty-five miles from shore. Receiving an urgent phone call that one of the children needed my help, I responded.

My friend ordered a helicopter from Bayou LaBatre, to rescue me so I could return to Georgia. That was quite an experience. One I shall never ever forget. It was nothing like the ride in Tupelo many years go.

My little black book was beginning to contain several names. Flowers began arriving at my office on a daily basis. I was being courted by men, and I wasn't as afraid as I had anticipated.

"HIM" agreed to meet me again. We met in a secluded spot this time. We talked for several hours. Our meetings were like a therapy session. "HIM" was a good listener. He also had numerous words of wisdom to convey to me. I listened and heeded his advice.

I told "HIM" of my dream. He recommended that I join another church and get involved. Aunt Katie had also made the same suggestion. I followed up, and began attending the Cave Spring United Methodist Church.

The pastor, was a young man. All of the members were so congenial and welcomed me with open arms. Immediately I was asked to interpret the church services. I was back on course.

The children continued to be estranged from me. I had not seen Mother since January. I had made a vow never to see her again.

I mentioned this often at church, and requested the prayers of the congregation. The membership of that little church treated me as if I were part of their family. It reminded me so much of Nettleton, and the Methodist Church that I attended as a child.

Church members Pete Housch and Dennis encouraged me often. I was informed if I needed anything, to please call on them. Needing some repair work done at my house, I did just that. They obliged.

Dennis arrived early one morning, prepared to install the doorbell. I informed him that I must be cautious about a married man being in the house with me alone. Therefore, I went next door to visit my neighbor and good friend Navaughnia Kerr.

In my absence, Dennis began the chore of placing the doorbell above the door in my bedroom. During the process, my talking clock announced the hour of the day.

Unaware that I had such a clock, Dennis thought that I had returned, and he had not seen me as I entered the house. He began to look for me. Exiting the house, he spied me across the yard at Navaughnia's. When I saw him in the yard, I thought he had completed the repairs, therefore I returned home.

He then informed me that he had heard a voice, very clearly in my house. I began to laugh. It was the first time that I had laughed since my husband's departure. Bending double with laughter, and with tears streaming down my face, I directed him to the bedroom to show him the clock.

Relieved that I had not been invaded by ghosts, he resumed his work.

Later, regaining his composure, he said that he had heard rumors in town that we had a friendly ghost living in our house. Admitting to the fact that we had held those suspicions also, I related another story.

The previous owner of our house, was married to an avid fisherman. He not only loved to fish, he dearly adored the cabin. He was disappointed when she sold it to us.

The former owner never returned to the house after we moved in. Two years later he died. We felt that his spirit had lived on within the house. Often when things were missing, or there was something wrong, we blamed it on the friendly ghost.

One day I scolded my child for being too close to one of his dates. While they were sitting on the couch nearby, I arose to go to the kitchen for refreshments for the two, the cover on the overhead light immediately fell into the chair where I had been sitting.

The person was naturally startled. My child and I both laughed at the sight of the broken glass and immediately blamed it on our friendly ghost. The young man became very cautious around our house following that frightening episode.

Laughing as he left, Dennis promised to bring me a load of firewood. There had been a recent storm in Cave Spring, and several old trees had been blown down. Dennis and several others had volunteered to clean up the debris and donate the wood to those in need. I was one of the recipients of the donated wood that year.

Often, I would pray for needs to be met. I knew nothing about operating the Snapper riding lawn mower. One of my boys volunteered to come and instruct me in the proper operation of the huge machine. Succeeding in the training, I began to mow my own lawn.

"HIM" and I continued to talk on the telephone. We would meet as often as we could, in various public places, so as not to be detected. It was definitely a time of transition for me. I fought diligently the urge to fall in love with him. But I dared not. I could not afford to mar my reputation at this stage in life.

At "HIM's" insistence, I began to exercise and walk. Daily, I would park my car at the end of Bluff Road, walk the six miles home, then return later to retrieve my automobile. I was beginning to shape up.

By now, I weighed one hundred and three pounds and was

into a size three dress. My weight had plummeted from over two hundred pounds, a dress size of 22 1/2 to the present weight and into petite size dresses. I needed a new wardrobe, but could not afford it.

Frequenting yard sales, and the Salvation Army, I began to accumulate nice clothing. Navaughnia is an excellent seamstress and serves as my tailor. She spent many hours at altering my clothes. I felt good about myself and the way I looked in my new wardrobe.

Navaughnia and Sam Kerr are wonderful neighbors. They have been living near us for more than fifteen years. I poured my heart out to her many a day during my hours of loneliness.

Sam was always ready and willing to assist me if I needed help. He is a man of a dying breed. The kind of man a person can call on at any time, day or night. I felt comfortable and protected on Sleepy Hollow even though I was alone in my own home. Knowing that Sam and Navaughnia were watching, I was not afraid. Lonely but not afraid.

Early one morning, in a rush to get to the office on time, I inadvertently backed over the mailbox. Hurriedly, I exited the car to assess the damages. Realizing that I must find someone to repair it, I continued on my way to work.

That afternoon, after work, I parked my car, and walked the six miles home as usual. When rounding the curve on Sleepy Hollow, I spied the upright mailbox. It had been replaced, and was secured tight within the ground. Gravel had been placed around the foot of the pole and the stones replaced in neat order.

I could not imagine who had done the repairs, because I had not mentioned the downed mailbox to anyone. Later, during the week, I made a visit to Navaughnia's and Sam's. That was when I discovered that "Good ole Sam" had observed me leaving that morning and saw me hit the mailbox. He was the good Samaritan who helped me that time.

Often, I would pray for my needs to be met. I had been accustomed to a two paycheck household, now I was footing the bills alone. It was a tight squeeze by any man's standards.

On numerous occasions, I would stop by to get my mail from the post office box in town, to find that someone had placed some cash in an envelope and mailed it to me. I could never identify the handwriting on the outside of the envelope.

I considered it a gift from God. He was answering all my prayers in such rapid succession, that it was almost unbelievable.

I am a firm believer in prayer, but this was more than I had ever experienced in all of my entire life.

One day, by sheer coincidence, I contacted a local garage to have my car serviced. The person who answered the telephone had a voice similar to the one I heard in my dream. Excitedly, I made arrangements to have them check my car.

The person who answered the phone had a name similar to the name "Chuck." He loved to dance, and was a member of the Legion. He was a divorcee, attractive, and was considered an excellent dancer. We made a date for Friday night.

With wild anticipation, I looked forward to Friday night. I had not danced in years, and was really looking forward to this time.

At the Legion, we danced until closing. I was tired but happy. Another dream had come true.

Fighting off the possibility of falling in love, I had to be cautious about my relationship. C. enjoyed dancing. I enjoyed dancing, but that was the extent of anything else we had in common.

By now it was Mid-August. I did not want to dance anymore, I was now interested in other things.

"HIM" and I continued to chat on the telephone. We agreed to meet for a short period out of town. I was frightened as to what might materialize. My divorce had not been finalized, in fact my husband had yet to file for it. I began to wonder if he was having second thoughts.

I drove the sixty miles where I had consented to meet "HIM" at a restaurant. We sat in the parking lot and talked for a while. Then we went inside to have dinner. I felt very uncomfortable. It was as if I were a thief and had stolen property in my possession.

"HIM" was not too tall. He in no way resembled my spouse. A good conversationalist, he kept me entertained with his war stories. We talked for a while, then he said that we must discontinue to see or talk to each other. I knew that this time would eventually come, however I was unprepared. I began to cry.

Making an attempt to console me, he said it was for the best and that he had made a mistake by leading me on. He would soon be out of my life, just like my first true love. It was almost more than I could bear.

Exiting the restaurant, without completing our meal, amid the stares of all the customers, I walked briskly to my car. "HIM" followed and stopped beside the driver's side where I sat in tears.

He asked if he could kiss me. This was out of character for "HIM." He had never made any advances toward me sexually, not even to place his arm around me, much less caress me.

Reluctantly, I consented. As our lips touched, it acted as a seal of our affection for each other. I knew without a doubt when we kissed, that he would have been an excellent lover. I would not and could not ever let myself resort to relinquishing my body for a few moments of stolen pleasure.

"HIM" was not mine, nor would he ever be. God had someone else in store for me, and I knew this.

As I drove away, I watched him as he strolled across the parking lot toward his automobile. "HIM" would no longer be a part of my life. I must rest assured that the Lord was sending someone real soon to fill this void.

MY THANKS TO "HIM"
by
Doris Isbell Crowe

You came along when I was sad
And made me laugh again.
You gave me hope and faith to go
To strive toward the best I can.

You gave me strength to carry on
When I was down and blue.
It was because of all your care
That this tribute is to you.

You'll never know the joy I had,
When first I saw your face.
I felt myself become alive
In another time and place.

The hours we talked and shared our thoughts
About the trials of life.
You'll never know, how much it meant
To clear myself of strife.

Now that you're gone, I'm not alone
I have a man of Dreams.
And you my dear, will be so near
In my heart it seems.

But I did care and I did know
That you were not the one
That I should have to hold and love
Until the rising sun.

But ne'ertheless, you still were there,
When one I did really need.
I'll always too, remember you,
And all your kindly deeds.

And now you're gone, I miss you too,
But it was not to be.
But rest assured from now till then
You meant the world to me!

    I visited Alisha on numerous occasions. Careful not to visit when Dennis was asleep, or when he was present.
    Dennis and I were good friends and could converse on the same level, but I was fearful of what people might think, if they saw me making too frequent visits to the Mason residence. Beth was still overseas at this time, and Alisha continued to need some sort of support.
    August was the birthday of my children's father. He had returned to Georgia and had asked someone to call me to see if I was at home. He wanted to talk. I consented to see him.

When he arrived, late that afternoon, he was surprised at the weight I had lost. He commented on how good I looked. He also asked for a trial reconciliation. I personally felt that the only motive that he had in returning was that he had no place to live.

Recalling the freedom that I had experienced during the summer, the people I had met, the obstacles that I had overcome without him, I declined his offer. I had joined the world of the hearing and was fully enjoying every minute of it.

When he left that evening, I went to my diary, and read all of the notes that I had written in his absence. I also sifted through all of the evidence that I had prepared for my defense in the divorce proceedings. I prayed a little, cried a little and became more and more angry by the minute. To think that this man could be so callous as to walk out on me when I needed him most, then come back when he needed me, was more than I could bear.

The following Saturday, we all attended our granddaughter's birthday party. Her granddaddy was in attendance. Following my review of the materials the night before, and viewing all of the information that I had in my briefcase, the report from the private investigator, and the letters in my possession, made me have strong and bitter feelings toward him.

I knew in my heart that I still had some love for him. I knew also that I would always have the memories of our life together. The memories of times that I had trusted him. With a gnawing feeling in my bosom, I felt I could never put my trust in him anymore.

Dennis telephoned that evening after the party and asked if I would be attending church the following day. Puzzled at his question, I responded with a yes.

He then informed me that he had someone he wanted me to meet. The man was a co-worker and would be accompanying him to church. I did not really relish the thought because I was still experiencing mixed emotions regarding "HIM" and my soon to be ex-husband. However, I consented to meet the man. Dennis did not give me any details about the man I was to meet, so basically it would be a blind date.

Surprisingly enough, I had dated several men during the

summer, but had not dated one single deaf man. I had no desire to continue in the world of the deaf.

Sunday morning dawned, a beautiful day. It was hot and muggy, as usual, I dressed prepared to interpret for the deaf at church. I would be moving my membership to this little church that day.

25.
LOUIE ALLEN CROWE

Rising early as usual, I exercised vigorously for about an hour. Choosing a dress that would make me look stylish, I left to meet the man selected by my good friend Dennis.

Upon entering the church, I greeted the Dillards. They were always present, and were so complimentary of my interpreting for them. I had always loved them, but loved them even more, now that I was alone. Then I saw the stranger seated in the pew next to Dennis.

Church services had not begun, and rising from his seat, Dennis motioned for me to come and meet his friend.

The man he had brought to church to meet me stood to greet me. He was tall and had curly reddish brown hair. He appeared to be approximately forty years of age. His smile was contagious and his demeanor very polished. Dressed in a white coat, he looked very distinguished among the other members of the congregation. As he stood to greet me, Dennis introduced us. He said "This is Doris McDonald, the lady I told you about." Turning to the gentleman, he introduced me to him. His name was Louie Allen Crowe, but Dennis had introduced him as Louie. That was the name he was called at Inland Rome, Inc., where he worked as a Power Operator. The date was August 26, 1990. Following the introductions, Louie responded, "I'm happy to meet you."

The voice! I knew it! It was the voice of the man in my vision. I could hardly believe it! My mind raced frantically. The happenings of the past week seemed to fade away immediately.

This was the man God had sent to me. I knew without a doubt in my mind. There was a definite spiritual bond present.

The song service began. I glanced toward Louie and Dennis. Louie's eyes were glued on me. I said a silent prayer. "Lord, if this is the one, help me to impress him, and guide me until I catch him."

All during the service, as I stood to interpret, I could feel Louie's watchful eyes on my hands as I interpreted. Smiling occasionally, I would look their way. He was a handsome man. He resembled a doctor I knew in Rome. Immediately, I liked him.

Following the church service, I joined the Methodist congregation as planned. Louie joined the other members in welcoming me. As he shook my hand, he said, "You have a wonderful ministry here and it's obvious the Lord has anointed you to do His work."

The voice! I knew it was the same one. Shaking like a leaf, I shook his hand. It was difficult to contain my composure, but I knew that I should. He had been told that I was a lady, and I must conduct myself as such.

However I wondered about him. If he was so fine, why was he not married? Had he experienced a similar traumatic divorce? Was he widowed? What did he know about the deaf? Would he understand "my world?" Did he have children? How many and how old were they? Did he have any sisters or brothers? Were his parents still living? What would he think of my children, and the fact that they had abandoned me?

What would he think of me and my relationship with my own mother? Was he an everyday Christian or just a Sunday Christian? Did he smoke? Did he drink? Did he curse? What did he think of me? Was I too short for him? Did he find me attractive? Did he like my hair? Did he like the things that I liked? Would he like Sleepy Hollow, or did he like city life? Was he a hard worker or was he lazy? Was he a good listener like "HIM?" Was he pushy or bossy? Did he sleep late in the morning or go to bed late at night? Did he like sports? Did he like music? Could he sing? Could he play an instrument? Did he have money, or was he poor? Could he tolerate someone who was talkative or did he prefer someone who was quiet? Did he like mission work, or did he find that boring? Was he patient and kind? Did he like the water? Did he like to travel? Did he like flea markets? Did he like to shop? Did he like to walk and exercise like I did? Could he tolerate a hyperactive woman who loved life? Did he enjoy humor? Was he thoughtful and did he readily give gifts? Did he remember special occasions? Did he like to read? Did he like crossword puzzles? Did he like to watch T.V.? Did he like to attend parties, weddings and receptions?

In a matter of a few minutes, these questions raced through my mind. Could I settle for half of them or not?

With all the questions still on my mind, Dennis invited me to join them at Todd's, a local restaurant, for lunch. We were to ride in Louie's automobile.

Opening the door to the passenger's side, I slid into the seat of his Mitsubishi. His Bible lay on the driver's seat. He had gone around the car to open the door for Dennis.

I began to open his Bible and thumb through it. It was marked on almost every page. This man of God was the one in my vision.

To my amazement, Louie Allen Crowe, was sixty years of age. It was very difficult to believe because he looked so young and vibrant. In addition, he had very few wrinkles on his face. He appeared to be a rather quiet man, but on the other hand he impressed me as a person who could be outspoken if need be.

The three of us journeyed on to the restaurant to have lunch. I was certainly anxious to become better acquainted with this nice man. I liked his mannerisms, and we appeared to be compatible.

By now, I knew in my heart he was a Christian and a strong stalwart man of God. He believed in prayer. I knew, because before we left the church parking lot, he had prayed with one of the church members who had just recently undergone heart surgery.

Inside the restaurant, we located a vacant booth. It was now time for "twenty questions." My first words to him were, "Mr. Crowe, I want it understood that I classify myself as a lady, and I expect you to treat me as such. If you dare to touch me in any way unbecoming to a lady, you will promptly draw back a nub."

Startled at such strong words being emitted from such a tiny lady, he chuckled. Crossing his arms, he said that I had nothing to fear and he would definitely remember that.

He was most definitely shocked to hear a statement like this from one who had just less than an hour ago stood in the church and interpreted for the deaf. Nevertheless, he was convinced that I fit the description that Dennis Mason had given of me.

The previous evening, Dennis had approached him at work and asked if he was divorced. Louie responded that he was, and that at present was not dating anyone.

Dennis, his supervisor, then asked if he was interested in meeting a lady. Louie's response was an affirmative yes! He replied also that he had met a lot of "trash" in his time, and he would like to meet a lady.

The questioning began. I inquired of him, each thought that had raced through my mind earlier that morning.

An interesting man, he was also very versatile. I was pleased at Dennis' selection for this "blind date."

Deciding to leave us alone to talk. Dennis left. He would be leaving for work at Inland Rome shortly. Louie was scheduled to work the same shift, so we did not have much time to converse today.

Hoping and praying that this would not be the last time that I had the opportunity to talk with him, I asked if he would like to drive out to my house on Sleepy Hollow Road. He consented.

As I drove through town, I recalled that my hearing had improved greatly following the stroke. Another contributing factor was the loss of accumulated fluid I had retained prior to my weight loss. I was now only wearing one hearing aid. My hands revealed very little atrophy from the stroke of a year and a half ago. However, I still had difficulty in eating and swallowing.

A straw was required, when I drank, to prohibit the liquids from falling from the corner of my mouth. I still experienced some numbness on one side of my face. My fingers on my left hand were not as nimble as those on my right hand. I could play the organ, but experienced much difficulty in playing the keys on the piano.

I prayed all the way from Cave Spring to Sleepy Hollow. I did so want to impress this man. I was convinced he was the man from God.

Many thoughts raced through my mind during the seven mile trip.

My soon to be ex-husband had filed for the divorce the day following his birthday, and the designated date for finalizing was September 3, 1990. I was not looking forward to the event at all, but he was still on my mind.

Arriving, prior to Louie, I hurriedly straightened up the den, dusted both the piano and organ, and waited for him to arrive.

He had removed his coat and tie prior to entering the house, so he looked more relaxed than he had several hours earlier. We had only two hours to talk and get to know each other.

I had discovered in my "twenty questions" routine that he loved everything that I did. EVERYTHING! Incredible. Either this man was the biggest con man combination liar that I had ever met, or he was Mr. Right. Deep in my heart, I knew it was the latter.

We chatted for a few minutes than we moved to the organ. He informed me that he owned both an organ and a piano. However, he could not play either, very well. He was in the process of taking music lessons. In addition, he took voice lessons on a regular basis and was armed with two suitcases of music.

He then proceeded to return to his automobile to retrieve his collection of books, and sheet music. We selected some songs that we both knew. As I played the organ, he began to sing. Harmonizing, I joined in with my alto voice. Following our musical duo, and choking back tears, he looked at me and reiterated that I must be anointed of the Lord to have such a variety of talents. Beginning to enjoy his company, more and more, we began to talk about our families. I was real comfortable with him from the very beginning of our meeting.

Looking at his watch, he informed me that he must leave for work. He then requested that I play the piano. Reluctantly, I moved to the piano bench. I began to play one of the beloved old hymns. My fingers moved across the keys as nimble as a child's. The atrophy was no longer prevalent. Somehow, I had been miraculously healed that very day. The day that I met Louie Allen Crowe.

Saddened to see him depart, he reassured me that he would call me. Within an hour, he had telephoned from his work. He could not talk long, but just wanted to thank me for a good time. He was very polite and had exquisite manners.

Later in the afternoon, I received a call from Dennis, requesting that I check on his step-daughter. He also asked my opinion of Louie. Naturally my response was, "Where have you been hiding him all this time?" Laughing at the excitement in my voice, he said, it was his policy to always save the best until the last. At that moment, that was my true feeling also.

Louie called six more times that night. He agreed to have lunch with me the following day, in Cedartown, before going to work.

Prior to my meeting Louie, I had not been eating regular meals. Still dieting and exercising, I usually feasted on diet colas and cereal.

One of my sons appeared to be concerned about me, and began to call periodically. His wife, would call also to see how I was doing. I then informed them of Louie. They wanted to meet him. I too, was anxious for them to meet this nice man.

The grandchildren, upon meeting Louie began to call him "Wooeie." He was an instant hit with both of them. I knew that he would be, there was no doubt in my mind.

Following the introductions to my family, it was my turn to meet his family.

On one occasion, he informed me that his mother was still alive at age 82, and still resided in the home place in Rome. I was very anxious to meet her. I was also curious as to how she looked.

The day arrived for us to visit his mother. One of his two sisters would also be visiting, so I had the opportunity to meet both of them simultaneously.

I had begun to call Louie Allen, "Baby." His pet name for me was "Precious." He would always say you are my darling, precious whenever he phoned me. I anxiously awaited his phone calls each day.

"Baby" and I arranged for a late afternoon meeting of his two relatives. I was somewhat nervous, but confident that everything would be ok. I prayed that they would like me.

Mrs. Dolla Cape, Allen's mother, stepped off the porch to greet us. I was shocked. Another prayer had been answered. God is so good.

"Nana" as she was affectionately known, was the epitome of Mommie. It was remarkable at the resemblance between the two. She even talked like Mommie. A prayer warrior, Bible-reading, kind-hearted, church-going, family-oriented, loving woman, she was another answer to my prayer.

We embraced. It seemed as if we had known each other for years, and that she knew all about me. She even treated me like Mommie did. I felt so comfortable and at home in her little neatly kept household. Later, Allen's younger sister, Jerry Oakes, joined us. Accompanied by her granddaughter Jennifer Hillman, she bore some resemblance to Allen. She was a lover of music also. A pianist in the local church, she was known for her beautiful alto voice. Not having had the opportunity to hear her sing, I had been informed that she was in great demand as a vocalist for weddings, funerals and other occasions within the Rome area. I liked her immediately. She, like Nana, made me feel a part of the family instantly. It seemed that we had known each other for years, and I was just coming for a visit.

Naturally, I related my "Vision" story. The story following, came from "Nana." She said that she and Allen had been praying for someone to be a helpmate to him. Someone who could play an instrument and sing with him. A person who was dedicated, and would assist him in continuing the Nursing Home Ministry that the Lord had laid on his heart. I, too, was an answer to their prayer.

September 3, 1990 arrived. One of my good friends, agreed to accompany me to the divorce proceedings. I had cried some then prayed some the night before. I felt that the Lord was leading, and He was helping me in this decision. I was following in His footsteps.

The divorce finalized, it would be advertised in the local newspaper the following Monday. Everyone would then know for certain that the man who was deaf was no longer a part of my life.

I had been awarded the van, automobile, and the house on Sleepy Hollow. Not asking for alimony, we had planned an amicable divorce, but it was not to be. The year following the divorce would be evidence of that statement.

MY DEAREST NANA
by
Doris Isbell Crowe

I see you now this very day
As you are growing old.
I did not know you way back when,
Your hair was brightest gold.

I know for sure that as each day
The sun comes into view,
That it was God who led the way
For me to come find you.

I'd prayed before while on the floor
For "Mommie" to return.
God heard and answered all my pleas,
Now no more do I yearn.

To have a good and saintly one
On whom I can rely.
One who will listen to my cares,
Then comfort me when I cry.

You are the one that helps me so
And oft warms me with your coat.
You are the one that always says
"Sit steady in the boat."

And now today as this I write,
I want the world to know
That you are the sweetest of Moms,
And I dearly love you so!

When Allen Crowe entered my life, a whole new world evolved. I had never had the experience of sitting in the swing on the solarium in the dark, especially with a hearing man's arms around me.

Allen could make me laugh so hard I would cry. He dearly

loved to imitate Amos and Andy, a comic duo from an old radio show. His accent was so comical, and the dialogue that he had developed was even funnier.

I often wondered if the neighbors could hear me laughing, and were curious as to what was occurring next door to make me so amused.

Allen loved music. We would turn on the stereo, listen to the songs and sing along with the vocalist.

In the afternoons, we would often go to a restaurant in Cave Spring, and choose our favorite songs on the jukebox. We were like two teenagers in love. He would look deep into my eyes, hold my hands and sing along with the recordings. Spending quarter after quarter, we would sit in a booth, until closing time.

The teenagers in town, I am sure, laughed at the old fogies and their crazy antics. We were very much in love and it was obvious.

He sent flowers, brought me little gifts, and took me shopping to the mall. His favorite place to eat was Po Folks in Rome. We became regular customers there, and were recognized instantly when we entered the restaurant. I, too, could let him give the waitress our order. No longer was I required to be the ears and mouth of the person accompanying me.

Allen could whisper sweet nothings in my ear. He could even become mushy on the telephone. Overhearing gossip from other workers, he could tell me what was happening around him. Often, if he heard a news special, or some special occurrence on the radio, he would telephone to inform me.

Being with Allen, a hearing man, was so much different than being in the company of a man who was deaf. There were no lights to inform him of the telephone or doorbell ringing. It was not necessary for him to rely on a telecaptioning device to understand the dialogue on the television.

If he was down at the creek watching the fish, it was not necessary for me to go all the way down there to get his attention. I could just yell, and he would hear me.

We could walk and talk in the moonlight along the shore near Brushy Branch. A light was not needed. Sitting on the front porch, we could hear the crickets and the frogs down at Carr's lake. He could hear me cough, laugh or even cry. There was no silence when he was around. We both lived in a sound oriented world.

Allen enjoyed singing with me. Our voices blended very well, and we harmonized whether I sang alto or tenor. I still enjoyed playing the piano or organ. Allen could sit and listen while I played. The enjoyment on his face far surpassed anything that I could describe. The sounds from my piano were no longer falling on deaf ears. He shared my joy of listening to the tunes as my fingers played each note.

The new sweethearts were on the go, dating every chance they got, and talking on the phone for hours.

Life was definitely different. We attended weddings, funerals, receptions, church and socials. It was not necessary for me to interpret for him. He could converse with his friends, and I could chat with the ladies.

Whenever he was visiting, he would answer the telephone. That had always been my responsibility before, even when the children were at home.

He could hear the doorbell, a knock on the door, or the dogs barking next door. Whenever we walked down Sleepy Hollow, he could identify the various birds and their mating call. He told me story after story.

One in particular, was the story of the Eagle. How the great bird takes its young from the nest, and holds it within its claws, then spreads its mighty wings and takes the tiny bird high into the air.

The majestic bird, then releases its offspring to fly alone. If it fails, then the Eagle, soars beneath the faltering one and it rides on the back of its mother, back to the nest. The Eagle performs this ritual until the young Eagle is strong enough to fly alone. Then it is left to go on to greater heights, sans mother.

It was a beautiful story, and I cried when he told it to me. Having never heard it before, I was impressed.

A TRIBUTE TO THE BIRDS
by
Doris Isbell Crowe

Did you ever see an Eagle
Spread its mighty wings to fly?
Did you ever see a sparrow
Soar swift across the sky?

Did you ever see a Red Bird
Gather food to take its young?
Did you ever see a Hummingbird
Suckle a redlight, then know something's wrong?

Did you ever see two gray birds
As they professed their love?
And did you look a little closer
To see that they were turtle doves.

Did you ever stop to think a while
That the birds and fowl of air
Could teach us many a thing or two
'Bout freedom, love and care?

Did you know that this old world of ours
Would be much better, oh by far,
If we could take some timely lessons
From the birds within the mar.

 Allen loved to read. He would often read to me as we rode in the automobile. I also enjoy reading, and would return the favor often, as we sat alone in the swing on the solarium. I was so happy. This was definitely a world that I had never known.
 Allen would sing love songs to me and quote poetry to me. Writing me love letters, and songs, I was beginning to feel like a Cinderella.
 October 15, 1990. Allen asked me to be his wife. With mixed emotions, I consented.
 We then went to a local jeweler to procure an engagement

ring. It was a beautiful one ct. diamond cluster, gold filigree, band. It was official.

We then planned the wedding. The month of June was mentioned first. The following day it was changed to May. Three days later it was changed again to March. A week later, it was moved up to December.

The final decision was for the festive occasion to occur December 15, 1990. I had never had a formal engagement, nor a church wedding. Allen decided that I should have both, to fulfill a dream. Two short months lay ahead until the day of the exchanging of vows.

We went to a local photographer, a long-time deaf friend, to have our pictures made. He had a little shop located in Cave Spring. There we had the engagement pictures made for the newspaper.

Upon seeing the engagement in the newspaper, the children wanted the things that I had been collecting for them.

Following the divorce, the most difficult chore that I had to perform, was sifting through memorabilia that I had accumulated through the years. At that time, I made certain that all of the children would receive the various items that we had designated for them. I cried even more at looking at old photographs. Happy times.

One child came to get the china, crystal, silverware, dinnerware, and the other collectibles that I had collected for a special day, their marriage. During October, we had planned for one of the boys' birthdays. At that time, we invited all of Allen's family, my children and Dennis. He had just returned from a trip to Greece to visit Beth, so he was in attendance also. My ex-husband came to join the festivities. We had an enjoyable time at the party. I was happy that the special occasions would continue, and that he and I could remain friends, or at least be on speaking terms.

Thanksgiving came, and we celebrated with Allen's family. It was at this time that I met Allen's other sister Faye, and her husband Pete Ryther of Marietta. I felt so comfortable with all of Allen's relatives.

My family chose not to visit us during this holiday. I was very disappointed, but tried to understand.

The wedding day was nearing. The solarium was filled with everything nameable in preparation for the big event.

My dress had been ordered, and Navaughnia had altered it to fit me to a "T."

My friends would help me decorate and assist in the catering of the wedding. This would save money, however, it would require more of my time to be devoted to the preparation of the entire affair.

My ex-husband stopped by late one afternoon following a school day. He wanted to wish me the best of luck. He also informed me that the children would not be attending the wedding, and he knew they felt I was remarrying too soon.

Telling him the story about the vision, he became very quiet. At the time he departed, I felt a strangeness about his presence. It was not at all like being with Allen.

Allen and I continued with our plans. One afternoon while we were addressing the invitations, he placed his arms around me. I was stunned at what he had to say. "I love you dearly, and always will, but if you feel that you need to be reunited with the one you loved before, I will reluctantly give you up. However, I will always love you."

26.
THE SECOND TIME AROUND

I began to cry. It had never entered my mind that I would want anyone other than Allen. He had opened up a new world for me and I could not visualize life without him, or his family.

December 15, 1990 dawned an overcast, dreary day. Everything was in order. The photographer and operator of the camcorder were in their respective places. The time for our wedding had finally arrived.

The following day, December 16, 1990, the Rome News Tribune, carried the following announcement on its society page:

"Dateline Cave Spring—Doris Isbell McDonald and Louie Allen Crowe were married at 2 p.m. Saturday, December 15 at the Cave Spring United Methodist Church. The bride is the daughter of Florence Isbell, Tupelo, Miss. and the late Carl

Morehead Isbell. The bridegroom is the son of Dolla Crowe Cape, Rome and the late Floyd Wesley Crowe."

The Rev. Keith Drew, Cave Spring, performed the double-ring ceremony before an altar decorated with a 15-branch heart-shaped candelabrum holding white tapers adorned with greenery, doves and red ribbon. The setting was completed by ceramic cherub angels and arrangements of poinsettias and magnolia leaves.

Music was presented by vocalist Jerry Cape Oakes, Rome, and organist Nancy Barker, Cave Spring. The interpreter for the deaf was Mary Ann Moncrief, Cave Spring.

Selections included "Love Me Tender," "What A Difference You've Made in My Life," "More," "Savior Like a Shepherd Lead Us," and "Welcome To My World." The processional was "The Bridal Chorus," and the recessional was "The Wedding March."

Alice Nelson McDonald, Rome, served as matron of honor and Teena Cagle, Cedartown, was the maid of honor.

They were attired in street-length dresses of teal green silk, each designed with a fitted bodice trimmed with a white collar adorned with embroidered angels on each side.

They carried cascading bouquets of white silk poinsettias with lace net adorned with green and cream ribbon streamers entwined with seed pearls.

Jennifer Hillman, Rome, was junior bridesmaid. She wore a red silk dress with a white collar.

The flower girl was Celisse McDonald, Rome.

The bride, given in marriage by Dennis Mason, Cave Spring, wore a two-piece tea-length dress of cream brushed satin. The Victorian-style dress was fashioned with Venice lace and featured a basque-style bodice with a choker collar of lace and a cameo insert on lace. The front and back necklined dipped to deep V-lines covered with matching lace and the long fitted sleeves were gathered with lace rosettes at the wrist. The drop waistline of gathered lace extended into a godet skirt of lace over satin.

She wore a double-tier shoulder-length veil of cream illusion held by a tiara headband. Silk flowers and pearls enhanced the headpiece and pouffes of illusion were featured on the back of the tiara.

The bride carried a cascading bouquet of white silk poinsettias, seed pearls, silk leaves and a silver ribbon resting atop a Bible, a gift of the bridegroom's mother.

The best man was Pete Ryther, Marietta. Ushers and candlelighters were Don McDonald, Rome; the Rev. Dewey Bailey, Cave Spring, and Nathan Oakes, Iceland.

The Ringbearer was Jordan Williams, Cave Spring.

The mother of the bridegroom wore a polka-dot fitted dress with a red linen jacket. Her corsage was a red green silk Christmas arrangement.

Beverly Williams wore a red silk dress and a corsage of white miniature silk poinsettias.

After the ceremony, a reception was held in the church fellowship hall. Refreshments included the bride's triple-tier column cake decorated with a bride and bridegroom music box and a flowing fountain.

Navaughnia Kerr, Cave Spring, kept the bridal registry. Servers were Beverly Williams, Beth Mason, Myrtle Dillard and Hattie Bailey all of Cave Spring; Susan Gattenby, Rome; Faye Cape-Ryther, sister of the bridegroom of Marietta; and Jean Sims of Pontotoc, Miss.

Birdseed bags were distributed by Jennifer Hillman, Celisse McDonald and Chelsey McDonald all of Rome.

After a wedding trip to Callaway Gardens, the couple will reside in Cave Spring.

On the evening before the wedding, Faye Cape-Ryther, Jerry Oakes and Dolla Cape hosted a dinner at Todd's Family House Restaurant in Cave Spring.

There had been several deaf people in attendance.

WE WERE OFFICIALLY MAN AND WIFE—now we were "The Crowe's."

ALLEN
I had a dream one night in June
About a fair-haired man.
He came to tell me not to cry
That joy was mine again.

I searched and searched, both high and low,
And all across the land.
To find the fair-haired one of my dream
And bring back . . . the other man.

But 'twas not to be that he'd be found
In any distant place.
For 'twas in my own home church
That first I saw your face.

Your curly hair and ready smile
Impressed me from the start.
And it was not too very long
Before you stole my heart.

And now that we are man and wife
I still remember clear.
The night I dreamed about a man
Who'd come and dry my tears.

You are the one and only one
That I could ever love.
Because I know without a doubt
You were sent from Heaven above.
Shalom.

27.
A NEW WORLD WITH THE HEARING

Following the wedding, we left for our honeymoon, I had joined the world of hearing. This honeymoon, I was certain, would be much different than the previous one. It was like an illusion the entire week we were gone. I was afraid that it was all a dream and I would soon wake up.

Our first stop was at the Westin Plaza Hotel in Atlanta. Allen was amazed that I wanted to play every musical instrument that I saw.

The following day, while at Macy's downtown store, a grand piano was located in the lobby. A pianist had been secured to provide Christmas music. When he had retired for the day, Allen asked if I would be allowed to play some music. Christmas shoppers stood on the balcony and observed us as we played and sang Christmas carols. The employees even joined in with us.

The following day we ventured to Callaway Gardens. Enroute, we stopped at a small Catholic church beside the road. I, of course, wanted to play the organ. The sister in residence allowed me to do so. I loved to play, Allen videotaped it, and often sang along with me. I was having a glorious honeymoon.

We returned to Sleepy Hollow Road to live. Plans were to move Allen's household furnishings into my place of residence. We also planned to remodel the exterior in the springtime. Typical of any newlywed couple, we had goals, expectations, and dreams.

The first week in January, I was informed that I no longer had a job. It was quite traumatic at first, but with Allen's assistance I knew that I would survive. Teena, Nancy and Dennis had supported me in my fight throughout all of my dilemma with the Mental Health Office. I felt that it must be God's will. This, like other disappointments that I had faced in life, would be just another stepping stone. Only this time I had a hearing mate to assist me. He stood beside me all the way.

We celebrated the New Year by attending a church function, then attending the Watch Night Service at the local First Baptist Church. We wanted to be in church to start the New Year of our marriage.

Three days later, we were involved in a serious automobile accident in Cedartown.

Dennis and Beth, who had by now returned from Saudi Arabia in time to attend the wedding, were planning to have dinner with us in Cedartown. Being distracted by my crying, after emptying my office of all my personal belongings, Allen inadvertently pulled into the path of an automobile. I was knocked unconscious.

Fortunately, Beth, who is a registered nurse, was immediately on the scene to assist in my care. I shall be forever indebted to her for being such a comfort to me at that time.

Allen was uninjured, but the new Camry had sustained several thousand dollars worth of damages. We were both disappointed, but thankful that the injuries that I had sustained were not too serious. We were both wearing seat belts and felt that it was the restraint of the belts that protected us from permanent scars.

The Lord once again had protected us from harm and provided good friends to be nearby to assist us in time of need.

We had to resort to using Allen's late model automobile. I was scheduled to be the official interpreter for the Governor's Inaugural Address at the Georgia Tech Coliseum in Atlanta, GA. Governor Zell Miller and Lt. Governor Pierre Howard were both friends of mine, and I felt very honored to serve in this capacity.

Two days prior to our leaving for Atlanta and the weekend activities of the inauguration, someone egged our automobile.

Allen was furious. We had suspicions that it might possibly be some of my family members, but we had no proof.

We called the police to investigate the incident. Naturally, it was printed in the newspaper. Another incident followed, where dead blackbirds were being thrown in our yard, and placed in our unused mailbox.

I even discovered a dead bird beneath one of the den chairs, when I attempted to move it while cleaning one Saturday. I began to panic. I called Navaughnia to be with me since Allen was at work. She came immediately to comfort me.

I was becoming a basket case. Some of my family members were even calling on the telephone and making outlandish accusations. Others were calling me derogatory names when they telephoned. I was so hurt by their actions. My new husband stood by me all the way.

My youngest child had made her wedding announcement. I knew that I would not be a part of her plans, nevertheless I prayed for her.

Gathering all the mementos that I had collected over the past twenty-one years, I placed them in a manila envelope. There was the new 1970 penny, from the week following her birth.

My mind raced back over the years to when I was a small child and had always dreamed of having a large wedding. My dad would escort me down the aisle to the tall man waiting for me at the altar.

That dream had just been fulfilled three months previously. I was very happy in my new life. I could only hope that my child could find the happiness that I had found and be content in her everyday life. I prayed each day for that happiness for her.

A small blue sachet powder container, trimmed in lace, was also included in the manilla envelope that I had prepared. There were several letters that I had written to her over the years at important times in her life. There was a letter written the night before informing her that I had made the decision not to attend her wedding. In addition there was some money to enable them to go to Florida for a week. I had been saving the bills for quite some time. There was something old, something new, something borrowed and something blue for my child, who could be marrying a child of deaf parents.

I left Sleepy Hollow at 11:00 a.m. to drive to Cave Spring to the post office, then to the parking lot of the church where she was to be wed to give the envelope to anyone who might be outside of the church. I felt assured they would give it to her.

It was not to be. The envelope was never delivered to her.

The following day, I drove by to visit with John, who had been in attendance at the wedding. At that time, my ex-husband presented me with the rose corsage that had been purchased for me to wear to the wedding. Without saying a word, I accepted it. The corsage remained in my refrigerator for two months. It was a daily reminder of my only daughter. Grief-stricken, I could not remove the thought of not attending her wedding, an occasion that both of us had planned for numerous times.

Finally, my best friend encouraged me to throw the rose away, and await another wedding to rejoice. That afternoon, I removed the wilted rose from the refrigerator, carried it to the end of Sleepy Hollow Road and gently buried it beneath the soil.

28.
MOTHER'S DAY

Mother's Day was approaching. I had not heard from any of the children, and hardly expected any of them to call, much less come for a visit. I would have been shocked if a card had arrived. Making attempts to prepare myself for being totally ignored on one of the most important days of the year for a mother, I tried to keep myself busy.

Allen was wonderful. He took me shopping and purchased me some White Diamonds perfume and powder. Daily, he would take me to a different restaurant to eat.

Four days prior to the day set aside to honor mothers, Allen took me to eat at Po Folks in Rome.

When we entered the restaurant, I spied a young woman seated at the next table. She was wearing the most beautiful cuff bracelet that I had ever seen. It was sterling silver, and was an enlarged replica of a dogwood blossom. Identical to the pattern on the ring that Judy Cook had given to me, many many years ago, I felt compelled to get a closer look.

I walked over to the lady, and inquired as to where she had acquired the strikingly beautiful bracelet. She informed me that she had purchased it in Cowpens, South Carolina, several years ago. I would dearly have loved to own a similar one to match my ring.

Returning to my seat, I commented on the beauty of the piece of jewelry. Shortly, the young lady, arose and came to our booth. She introduced herself. She was an employee at Inland Rome, Inc. She had recognized the logo on Allen's jacket.

Beginning to smile, she removed the bracelet from her arm and handed it to me. "You look like a good mother, and since it is nearing Mother's Day, I wish to give this bracelet to you as a memento for the day that is set aside to honor mothers."

In disbelief, I accepted it. This fine lady, not knowing the anguish I had been experiencing the past week, had just fulfilled a mother's wish. A wish that she would receive something special. That wish was granted. Once again, I thanked the Lord for his goodness to me. For intervening and comforting me when I was so discouraged. The bracelet was now mine to wear when I wore my silver ring.

My own mother had never had a visit from me on Mother's Day. I always celebrated my own, then the following week, I would visit her in Mississippi in the nursing home.

Mother had liked Allen the first time she met him. He was kind to her, even though he had not learned to communicate with her.

She was experiencing problems at the nursing home. In addition, she was gaining weight rapidly. Her feet were so swollen with fluids that she was unable to walk without the assistance of a walker in the home, and a wheelchair elsewhere.

We were informed that she was eating several bars of candy a day, and grieving over the fact that I did not visit more often.

Mother wrote to ask if she could come for a visit. Allen and I decided to bring her to Georgia for a short period of time.

TO MY DEAF MOTHER
by
Doris Isbell Crowe

You are the one who when so young
Gave me life at birth.
Who cared for me the best you could
And gave it all your worth.

It was no easy task while growing up
With a mother who could not hear.
Because I had to do so much
And be your listening ear.

But ne'ertheless, I did survive
The trials as they came.
I did endure, through many a day
And was proud to bear your name.

And now that you are getting old
Your hair is white as snow.
I know that it was meant to be
Jesus did love me, this I know.

Your deafness kept you from so much
Of life and all its dues.
But you, like those who follow you,
Will always make it through.

And I am glad that it is so.
You can now enjoy your life.
Away from all the cares and woes
Of troubles and of strife.

With pride and love and all the joy
Your daughter of today—
Can sign and talk to you
And understand each word you have to say.

As I, too, grow old and wrinkles show
I can truthfully say to you,
I loved you much, so very much,
For helping me make it through!

29.
A COWBOY WEDDING

    Meanwhile, John had announced that he would be marrying a long-time friend, Jackie Randolph. Jackie's mother and father were both deaf, and had visited often in my parents' home. In fact, her mother and I were pregnant at the same time.

    Jackie had two children by a previous marriage. A fifteen-year-old daughter, Kim Mills and ten-year-old Stephen Randolph.

    They were darling children. I adored them, and they adored me also. We were pleased at John's choice.

    A September wedding was planned, at the cabin near his home on the McDonald farm place. It would be a cowboy wedding, and a country music band would be there.

The wedding was beautiful. John sang Garth Brook's song, "If Tomorrow Never Comes" He sang with both his voice and in sign language. He has always been multi-talented, but he really showed it that day. All of the children were in attendance. Allen and I took Mother and she enjoyed herself.

Following the wedding, we brought Mother home with us. She liked Cave Spring so well that she wanted to move here.

We encouraged her to lose weight and begin an exercise program. Allen, now beginning to learn some sign language, encouraged her not to eat sweets. She listened to him. She began to walk without the walker. As time progressed, she lost sixty-eight pounds, walked two miles a day, and acquired a new wardrobe. Almost unrecognizable, she returned to the nursing home. However, she did not want to remain there. She wanted to move to Cave Spring and be near us.

We made application for Mother to move into an apartment in the local federal housing authority. There were no vacancies, so we consented for her to move into the house with us.

Two friends who had often assisted us in yardwork, Earl Montgomery and Steve Sheppard, assisted us in moving Mother from Tupelo, to Sleepy Hollow Road.

There were now three of us residing at the "Crowe's Nest." Mother began to really enjoy her new home. She was now enjoying life as it should be after retirement. She enjoyed being near family all the time.

Thanksgiving was coming and I was depressed that none of my family would be here. Allen encouraged me to invite his relatives and all of our friends. We had a house full of people. The house was filled with laughter and music all day.

Nancy and Jerry played and sang songs. My cousin Bert Jones and his wife Sue were present from Huntsville, Ala. My other cousin Jean Massengill-Becton Childers and her husband Buck Childers from Columbus were also present.

Our friends the Dillards; Dennis and Beth Mason; our neighbor Spencer Willis; Navaughnia; Nancy's mother Mrs. Tallulah Langston; Teena; Pete and Faye; Allen's niece Janie Hillman and her friend Steve; Jennifer Hillman and of course Nana.

Mr. Dillard entertained us with his antics and stories. Jean kept us laughing about her experiences in south Mississippi and Granny Massengill. It was a most memorable occasion.

30.
DONNA'S DEAF WORLD

I had planned to start back to school, possibly to nursing school. I decided to enroll at the local tech school for the fall term. There was a deaf student in attendance, Donna Smith Caldwell. She was needing an interpreter at the time, and I consented to assist her in her last year at Coosa Valley Tech.

Utilizing all the skills that I had gained over the years, I began to interpret for one of the brightest young deaf students that I have ever known. It was a joy to work with her. She was so enthusiastic and eager to learn, it was a pleasure just to see her smiling face each day.

Donna completed her studies, and I moved on. Donna will always remain in my memory as a deaf person who has taken advantage of all that life has to offer the deaf.

She, unlike my mother, will be able to raise her children in a deaf culture much different than the one that existed in the early forties.

Donna and Gary will have a doorbell light, telecaptioning for the television, a T.D.D. for the telephone, a light to inform them when their baby cries, and will have an interpreter provided by the local interpreting services. If they so desire, they can call an 800 number and converse with a hearing person via an interpreter, at no cost to them. She will have the advantage of the new federal laws that prohibit discrimination in hiring the handicapped. She will not have to settle for a menial job in a factory. Gary will be able to progress at the post office, and they will not have a "Dummy's Little Girl."

31.
THE CROWE'S NEST

Fall is nearing once again. Another school year. This year, 1992, I will be a full-time employee of the state as a houseparent at the Georgia School for the Deaf. At age 52, "Dummy's

Little Girl," has grown older. My mother will be 76 in September. Allen will reach his 62nd birthday in November. He will be eligible to retire from Inland Rome, Inc. before another year is completed.

Sam and Navaughnia are still our neighbors. The Joneses have long since moved away, and "Greasy Willis" is residing in their mobile home next door. He has built a new house just around the corner. I am told that my ex-husband is very happy and content in his deaf world. I see him occasionally around town on his Gold Wing motorcycle. The children are all fine and seem to be satisfied with their lives, work and their families. I have another granddaughter. Nana still lives alone in the old home place in Rome. I'll visit more often. Allen and I will continue to serve the Lord in our Nursing Home Ministry. His plans for the future include attending the Deaf Education program at Floyd College. In addition, we have applied for summer employment on a Christian cruise line, for the coming year. I have now completed the long awaited book.

It was through long hard hours, sheer perseverance, numerous tears, and mixed emotions that it was written, at Mary Frances Garrett's suggestion. Mother continues to peel peaches for me and to do the laundry. Maybe now we will have more time to spend together. We will go to Todds and Shumates to eat and Allen will play the jukebox for me like old times. Nancy, my very best friend, has not been well. But we still pray. We will still attend Live Oak Baptist Church, where I play the organ. Hopefully we will have a new paved parking lot this coming year.

I plan to resume my daily walks down Sleepy Hollow Road. The exercises will continue. The stairstepper's sound will be mingled with the noise of "Wheel of Fortune" each evening on television. The treadmill, thighmaster and the leg and arm weights will come alive. Uncle Otha passed away, Aunt Nannie, Aunt Eva Ruth, and Aunt Estelle all broke their hips. Uncle Bill died this past spring. Bubba still works with bees and his kids are doing fine. He lives in Tupelo. I plan to go to Nettleton every chance I have to ride around town. I also plan to go to the cemetery on my next visit. The yard at the Crowe's Nest will be mowed more often, and the flowers weeded.

Steve and Earl will continue to help us. The fire ants will be eradicated and the fish fed in the creek. I will make more visits to First National Bank of Polk County and take a little sunshine whenever I go. The house on Sleepy Hollow will get dusted more often, and the cobwebs swept down. Radio Shack employees can now rest! Gary won't receive any calls. Darryl will be in shock, because the Tandy computer will rest, but only temporarily. "HIM" is gone. Hattie and Dewey Bailey are still around. Connor and Myrtle Dillard still come for frequent visits. Mother enjoys Connor and his jokes. Allen is learning sign language well, Teena is still around, I talk to her on the phone often. Kristy is fine. Dennis and Beth are back home. Alyshia has two little boys now. Judy Cook Pryor and Jimmy are fine. Aunt Toy has a new home near Judy. Jean's husband Buck passed away in January of this year. Bert is still at Boeing in Huntsville. Aunt Winnie and Uncle Grif are now grandparents. John calls me often. Keith moved on.

The Crowe's Nest on Sleepy Hollow Road, I am confident, will buzz once again with the sound of laughter and family gatherings. Hopefully tears will not flow as freely as before. Also it is certain there will be more dreams. Inevitably, some failures will come and like other dreams before, some will come true.

Mommie will be affectionately remembered, and Dad will always have a soft place within my heart. He by no means was a dummy. Because of the new chapter in my life, I will no longer live in a totally deaf world. Allen brought the world of the hearing to me.

Because of Allen, he like the mighty eagle has ascended to the heights of the crest of the mountain with "Dummy's Little Girl." Just as the mighty bird does, he will place his strong protective wings around her and fly away. Then together he will allow her to soar to greater heights, some of which she has never seen. However, she will not fly alone, nor will she fly in silence. Unlike leaving the "Eagle's Nest," she will leave the "Crowe's Nest," side by side with a new mate. She will no longer endure hours of silence, or be relied upon to interpret for a deaf companion. It will not be necessary for her to serve as a "bridge over troubled waters."

"Dummy's Little Girl" served faithfully for more than fifty years as the ears, eyes, voice, and caretaker for someone who could not hear. She never knew what she had missed until someone in the "hearing world" showed her that true love, trust, and caring existed out there.

After experiencing that love, she could never return to the previous life that she once lived, therefore, "Dummy's Little Girl" will no longer exist.

EPILOGUE

TO ALL MY CHILDREN
by
Doris Isbell Crowe

I remember as a tiny tot
I loved my dollies dear.
But it wasn't long before my task
Was to dry my brother's tears.

As I grew a little older
And could babysit some kids,
I'd hope that in the future,
Mine would love me like they did.

God was gracious and He gave me
Four healthy little tykes.
Not a one was deaf, nor deformed,
But all could sing and ride their bikes.

I remember as I nursed you
Through each hour of every day,
That my thoughts were always of you,
But knew someday you'd go away.

I didn't know if God would call
You to His home in Heaven above,
Before you could find true happiness
With a mate you really loved.

I did not know for certain
That you would make it through
The many painful hours,
When illness came to you.

I did not know for certain
That you might have to go to war
And serve your mighty nation
On a foreign blissful shore.

I did not know for certain
If you would take a stand,
And go as a Missionary
To some far and distant land.

I do know now for certain
That I really loved you so.
And was more than just heart-broken
When you chose to leave, you know.

I haven't seen you children.
Nor heard from you so long.
I didn't know just what I said
Or did that was so wrong.

One thing I know for certain
That you're in my daily prayers.
And if you ever need me
I will always be right there.

To listen to your problems,
Comfort you when you are sad.
To help you get through trials
If things just get too bad.

I'll always love and care for you
Until my dying day.
But you'll never know the pain I've borne
Since you all went away.

The tears I've shed, the heartache too,
You'll never really know.
The loneliness that came at night
When I missed you so.

I asked the Lord to care for you
And bring you back to me.
He told me just to wait a while
And that He'd care for me.

So this to you, my children,
Whom I really love so much.
And pray and pray that some day
Again I'll feel your touch.

That I will hear you when you laugh,
And see you when you come
Up to my door and gently say,
Hey! Mamma, I've come home.

TEENA, A FRIEND ALWAYS
by
Doris Isbell Crowe

I'll ne'er forget the very day
When first your face I saw.
'Twas at our work in Cedartown
At that old school, Ha! Ha!

That very day I knew for sure
You'd be a lifetime friend.
One who'd share with me my ups and downs,
One on whom I could depend.

I've bent your ear on many a day
To share my cares and woes.
You always had good words to give
Even 'twas about my clothes.

You worried so that I'd not fail
In anything I tried.
Even when you were so filled with grief,
You gave me comfort when I cried.

I'll always be so thankful for
A friend who stood so firm,
When the whole world seemed a crashing down
At each and every way I turned.

So here's my thanks to you dear friend,
One on whom I'd always call.
You held me up when I was down
And refused to let me fall.

Your day will come, not far for sure,
Your "Knight in Shining Armor," too.
One fair of face, the fair-haired boy,
Will come and say "I do."

Until that day I'll hope and pray
You'll always remember me,
And how you helped a little friend
Become the best that she could be!

TO DENNIS, A VERY GOOD FRIEND
by
Doris Isbell Crowe

'Twas many, many years ago,
I came into Cave Town.
There were no seats at the ballfield,
And water was all around.

You, then were one who led the way,
To help whene'er you could.
The church, the town, the destitute,
And even those of widowhood.

The years have come and gone,
Our paths they rarely crossed.
Until one day, while on my way,
At the post office, I was engrossed.

You stopped to say a kind word or two,
To listen to my pleas.
Of little things that I needed done,
On Sleepy Hollow's trees.

I bore my soul to tell to you
How my heart had just been broken.
And you did list there for a while,
To each word that was spoken.

You befriended one, who at that time,
Was very blue and sad.
Your quick wit and ready smile
Attempted to make me glad.

As time passed by, your aiding hand
Was one on whom I could rely.
And if I made a call to ask of you,
You bade me not to cry.

I never shall forget the day
You told me of your friend.
Who was a kind and gentle man,
And on one I could depend.

You brought him to the little church,
To let me see 'twas true.
That he was good, a Christian man,
And considered real true blue.

You were not the kind to just give up,
And think that I might not bite
The bait that you had brought that morn,
For the fishing was just right.

The months did pass, you went your way,
And Louie was the one.
The man of dreams that I'd spoken of,
My search would all be done.

A wedding planned, you gave support
When I needed someone to care.
You, too, said that you'd give me away
To the one that was fair of hair.

So now as I am Mrs. Crowe,
I give my thanks to you.
For giving aid to a lonely one
Until she said "I do."

For your help in every way,
Your kindness ever shown.
You'll always remain that very close friend
'Til our days on earth are done.

THANKS NANCY!
by
Doris Isbell Crowe

I want to give you all the thanks
For things that you have done.
I don't believe I'd have made it through
'Til the battle had been won.

If not for you, on whom I'd call
To tell you all my ills,
I did not think that I'd make it through,
But you'd say, "Oh! But yes you will."

And now that you have been so weak,
I feel my helpless soul
Can't do as much for you, as you for me,
To help you reach your goal!

But everyday, I just kneel and pray
That God in Heaven above
Will strengthen you and cover you
With all the goodness of His love.

You are loved by everyone.
On you they have depended.
And we all know that it won't be long
Until your weakness is ended.

Then you can smile and go your way
To help some other brother.
Your light, brisk step within the halls
Will emulate your mother.

The day will come, I'm sure 'tis soon
That we will hear you say,
I know I'm healed, there is no ill,
I'm very well this day.

BUBBA
by
Doris Isbell Crowe

On one fine day, a way back when,
A brother came my way.
He was so small, so very small,
But I loved him that very day.

Our dad and mom, both so sure
Their kids were the very best.
And you, I thought, throughout my life
Were far superior to the rest.

Many a day has come and gone
Since our childhood days back home.
You went your way, I went mine,
But my love for you ne'er roamed.

As our hair turns gray and wrinkles creep,
I hope the memories never fade
Of a little boy and little girl
Who brought smiles to deaf ears that God made.

When we would sing and they would dance,
Play ball and cards and such.
A Momma and Dad who could not hear,
They loved us oh so much.

So here's to you, my first playmate
And the one who caught you when you'd fall.
May you always think of me as one
Who loved you first of all.

I love you...

           Sister.

DUMMY'S LITTLE GIRL
by
Doris Mae Isbell

Once in time a child was born
To a deaf man and his wife.
It fell her lot at an early age
To aid them in their life.

With nimble fingers she did convey
To parents, deaf by birth,
Each idle word, each uttered phrase,
To aid their walk on earth.

Even though so small, she stood so tall
To interpret the words to them.
As time passed on, a deaf man she wed
And remained faithful to sign for him.

Her fingers, tho', never wavered,
Told of God and all His love.
She, too, would sign for other deaf
As need be, come push or shove.

Doctors, pastors, lawyers, too
All sought the hands that signed out words.
As did teachers, moms and dads and
Vocalists emitting each and every chord.

She so willingly did go, whenever called,
To aid those who could not hear.
With swift and nimble fingers still,
After many and many a year.

She'll ne'er forget the deaf ones who
Did bring her to this world.
As a little child she was always known
As "Dummy's Little Girl."

GIFT SHOP

THE CROWE'S NEST
6 Broad Street
P. O. Box 854
Cave Spring, GA 30124
706-777-1439
Antiques - Jewelry - Candies